Securing Information in the Digital Age

Table of Contents

Securing Information in the Digital Age

By Roberto Miguel Rodriguez

Chapter 1: Introduction to Cybersecurity

The Importance of Cybersecurity in the Digital Age

In today's interconnected world, where technology is deeply integrated into every aspect of our lives, the significance of cybersecurity cannot be overstated. The digital age has brought about remarkable advancements and opportunities, but it has also given rise to new and sophisticated threats that target our digital infrastructure, networks, and information. This subchapter aims to shed light on the importance of cybersecurity and its implications for various stakeholders, including teachers, politicians, scholars, academicians, journalists, observers, and diplomats.

For teachers and academicians, understanding the importance of cybersecurity is crucial for preparing future generations to navigate the digital landscape. Educators must equip students with the knowledge and skills to protect themselves and their data online. By integrating cybersecurity into the curriculum, teachers can empower students to become responsible digital citizens and minimize the risks associated with cyber threats.

Politicians and diplomats play a vital role in shaping policies and regulations to safeguard national security and international relations. As cyber threats become increasingly sophisticated and pervasive, politicians must prioritize cybersecurity to protect critical infrastructure, government networks, and sensitive information. By investing in robust cybersecurity measures, policymakers can ensure the smooth functioning of society and maintain trust in government institutions.

Scholars and observers have the responsibility to conduct research and analyze trends in cyber threats to provide insights and recommendations. Their expertise can help identify vulnerabilities and develop effective countermeasures against emerging cyber threats. By disseminating their findings, scholars and observers can raise awareness and contribute to the collective effort of combating cybercrime.

Journalists, as information disseminators, have a significant role in reporting on cyber threats, breaches, and best practices. By providing accurate and timely information, journalists can educate the public about the risks associated with the digital age while also highlighting success stories and cybersecurity advancements.

For diplomats, cybersecurity is a critical aspect of international relations. As countries become increasingly interconnected, diplomatic efforts should include discussions on cybersecurity cooperation, information sharing, and tackling cybercrime. Diplomats must foster collaboration and establish norms and regulations to ensure a secure and stable cyberspace.

In conclusion, cybersecurity is of paramount importance in the digital age, affecting individuals, organizations, and nations at large. Teachers, politicians, scholars, academicians, journalists, observers, and diplomats all have a role to play in understanding and prioritizing cybersecurity. By collectively addressing this issue, we can mitigate the risks and protect our digital infrastructure, networks, and information from cyber threats.

Understanding Cyber Threats and Risks

In today's digital age, where technology plays a vital role in every aspect of our lives, it is crucial to be aware of the ever-evolving cyber threats and risks that can compromise our digital infrastructure, networks, and information. This subchapter aims to provide a comprehensive understanding of these threats, ensuring that teachers, politicians, scholars, academicians, journalists, observers, and diplomats can stay informed and take necessary precautions to protect themselves and their organizations.

Cyber threats are constantly evolving and becoming more sophisticated, posing a significant risk to individuals, businesses, and governments alike. These threats can take various forms, such as malware, ransomware, phishing attacks, social engineering, and advanced persistent threats. Understanding these threats is the first step towards mitigating the risks they pose.

Malware, or malicious software, is a common cyber threat that can infect computers, mobile devices, and networks. It includes viruses, worms, Trojans, and spyware, which can steal sensitive information, disrupt operations, or provide unauthorized access to systems. Ransomware, on the other hand, encrypts files and demands a ransom to restore access, causing significant financial and reputational damage.

Phishing attacks are another prevalent threat, where cybercriminals impersonate legitimate organizations to trick individuals into revealing sensitive information such as passwords or credit card details. Social engineering tactics exploit human psychology to manipulate individuals into divulging confidential information or performing actions that compromise security.

Advanced persistent threats (APTs) are highly sophisticated and targeted attacks that aim to gain unauthorized access to sensitive information or disrupt critical infrastructure. These threats often involve state-sponsored actors or organized cybercriminal groups and require advanced security measures to detect and mitigate.

To effectively address these cyber threats, it is imperative for individuals and organizations to implement robust cybersecurity measures. This includes regular software updates, strong and unique passwords, multi-factor authentication, encryption of sensitive data, and employee training on cybersecurity best practices.

Furthermore, collaboration and information sharing are crucial in the fight against cyber threats. Governments, businesses, academia, and individuals must work together to share threat intelligence, coordinate incident response, and develop innovative solutions to mitigate risks.

In conclusion, understanding cyber threats and risks is essential for teachers, politicians, scholars, academicians, journalists, observers, and diplomats operating in the digital age. By staying informed and implementing robust cybersecurity measures, individuals and organizations can protect their digital infrastructure, networks, and information from cyber threats. Together, we can create a safer digital environment and safeguard our society's progress and security.

Historical Overview of Cyber Attacks and Breaches

Introduction:

In the digital age, where information is the most valuable asset, the threat of cyber attacks and breaches has become increasingly prevalent. This subchapter aims to provide a comprehensive historical overview of cyber attacks and breaches, highlighting key incidents that have shaped the field of cybersecurity. It is essential reading for teachers, politicians, scholars, academicians, journalists, observers, diplomats, and anyone interested in understanding the evolution of cyber threats.

Evolution of Cyber Attacks:

The history of cyber attacks can be traced back to the early days of computing. In the 1980s, the emergence of personal computers and interconnected networks opened the doors for malicious actors to exploit vulnerabilities. The Morris Worm of 1988, one of the first notable cyber attacks, infected thousands of computers, causing widespread disruption and raising awareness about the need for cybersecurity measures.

The 1990s witnessed a surge in cyber attacks, with hackers targeting financial institutions, government agencies, and critical infrastructure. The infamous Love Bug virus in 2000, which spread rapidly through email systems, highlighted the vulnerability of interconnected networks and the need for stronger protection mechanisms.

Major Cyber Breaches:

The 21st century brought about a new era of cyber threats, marked by high-profile breaches that exposed sensitive information and compromised national security. The subchapter explores these significant breaches, such as the Stuxnet worm in 2010, which targeted Iran's nuclear facilities, and the Sony Pictures hack in 2014, which resulted in the leak of confidential data and created geopolitical tensions.

The subchapter also delves into the 2017 Equifax breach, one of the largest data breaches in history, where personal information of millions was compromised, emphasizing the need for stringent data protection regulations.

Lessons learned and the Future:

Throughout history, cyber attacks and breaches have demonstrated the ever-evolving nature of cyber threats. The subchapter concludes by highlighting the lessons learned from these incidents and the ongoing efforts in the field of cybersecurity.

It emphasizes the importance of international cooperation, public-private partnerships, and continuous investment in research and development to stay ahead of cybercriminals. Furthermore, it explores emerging technologies, such as artificial intelligence and blockchain, which hold the potential to enhance cybersecurity measures.

Conclusion:

The historical overview of cyber attacks and breaches presented in this subchapter provides a comprehensive understanding of the evolving threat landscape. It serves as a valuable resource for teachers, politicians, scholars, academicians, journalists, observers, and diplomats interested in the field of cybersecurity. By learning from past incidents, we can build a safer digital future and protect our critical infrastructure, networks, and information from cyber threats.

The Role of Politicians and Diplomats in Securing Information

In today's digital age, the protection of information has become a critical concern for individuals, organizations, and governments. As the world becomes increasingly interconnected, the importance of securing information cannot be overstated. This subchapter explores the vital role that politicians and diplomats play in safeguarding information in the face of ever-evolving cyber threats.

Politicians and diplomats, as key decision-makers and representatives of nations, have a responsibility to address the challenges posed by cyber threats and ensure the security of their countries' digital infrastructure, networks, and information. They possess the authority and influence to develop and implement robust cybersecurity policies and strategies.

One of the primary roles of politicians and diplomats in securing information is to understand the landscape of cyber threats. They must stay informed about the latest trends, technologies, and tactics employed by cybercriminals and state-sponsored hackers. This knowledge equips them to make informed decisions and develop effective countermeasures.

Furthermore, politicians and diplomats are responsible for establishing international collaborations and diplomatic engagements to combat cyber threats. Cybersecurity is a global concern that requires coordinated efforts among nations. Through diplomacy, politicians and diplomats can foster trust, share intelligence, and promote the adoption of common cybersecurity standards and best practices.

Another crucial role of politicians and diplomats is to advocate for the development of robust legal frameworks and regulations that address cyber threats. They must work closely with legal experts to draft legislation that criminalizes cybercrime, protects citizens' privacy rights, and enforces penalties for those who engage in malicious activities online.

Politicians and diplomats also play a pivotal role in raising awareness about cybersecurity among the general public. They can leverage their platforms to educate and mobilize citizens, businesses, and other stakeholders on the importance of adopting secure practices in their digital lives. By fostering a culture of cybersecurity, politicians and diplomats contribute to the overall resilience of their nations.

In conclusion, politicians and diplomats have a significant role to play in securing information in the digital age. Their ability to understand cyber threats, foster international collaborations, develop legal frameworks, and raise awareness is crucial for protecting digital infrastructure, networks, and information. By fulfilling their responsibilities, politicians and diplomats contribute to creating a secure and resilient digital environment for their citizens. This subchapter aims to provide insights and guidance to teachers, politicians, scholars, academicians, journalists, observers, diplomats, and anyone interested in the intersection of cybersecurity and politics.

Chapter 2: Fundamentals of Cybersecurity

Defining Cybersecurity and Its Scope

In an era defined by rapid technological advancements and widespread digitization, the concept of cybersecurity has become more critical than ever before. As our reliance on digital infrastructure, networks, and information increases, so does the need to protect these assets from the ever-evolving landscape of cyber threats. This subchapter aims to provide a comprehensive understanding of what cybersecurity entails and its scope in today's digital age.

Cybersecurity, in its simplest form, refers to the practice of protecting computer systems, networks, and data from unauthorized access, attacks, and damage. It encompasses a wide range of strategies, technologies, and policies aimed at safeguarding digital assets against cyber threats, which include hacking attempts, data breaches, malware infections, and other malicious activities. However, the scope of cybersecurity extends far beyond the realm of technology, as it also involves addressing the human, legal, and ethical dimensions associated with securing information in the digital realm.

For teachers, politicians, scholars, academicians, journalists, observers, and diplomats, understanding the intricacies of cybersecurity is crucial for several reasons. Firstly, it allows them to grasp the potential consequences of cyber threats on various sectors, such as national security, economy, healthcare, and personal privacy. By comprehending the scope of cybersecurity, these individuals can evaluate the potential risks and develop informed policies, strategies, and solutions to mitigate them effectively.

Moreover, this subchapter will delve into the specific niches within cybersecurity. For instance, it will explore the field of network security, which focuses on safeguarding computer networks from unauthorized access and ensuring the confidentiality, integrity, and availability of data transmitted through these networks. It will also shed light on information security, which concerns protecting sensitive information from unauthorized disclosure, alteration, or destruction.

Furthermore, the subchapter will address the emerging field of cybersecurity in the context of diplomacy and international relations. With the rise of state-sponsored cyber attacks and the increasing interconnectedness of nations, diplomats and observers need to understand the geopolitical implications of cybersecurity. They must navigate the complex landscape of digital warfare, cyber espionage, and the protection of critical infrastructure.

In conclusion, this subchapter aims to provide a comprehensive overview of cybersecurity and its scope in the digital age. By exploring the multifaceted nature of cybersecurity, it equips teachers, politicians, scholars, academicians, journalists, observers, and diplomats with the necessary knowledge to navigate the challenges and opportunities presented by the ever-evolving cyber landscape. Ultimately, understanding cybersecurity is not only crucial for protecting digital assets but also for ensuring the stability, security, and progress of our societies in the digital era.

Types of Cyber Threats and Attack Vectors

In today's interconnected world, where information flows freely and technology drives every aspect of our lives, the threat landscape has evolved, giving rise to a multitude of cyber threats and attack vectors. This subchapter aims to provide an overview of the various types of cyber threats that individuals and organizations face, as well as the attack vectors employed by malicious actors.

1. Malware Attacks: Malicious software, commonly known as malware, is designed to disrupt, damage, or gain unauthorized access to computer systems. This includes viruses, worms, trojans, ransomware, and spyware. Malware attacks can exploit vulnerabilities in software or trick users into downloading infected files.

2. Phishing and Social Engineering: Phishing is a deceptive technique used by cybercriminals to obtain sensitive information, such as passwords, credit card details, or social security numbers, by impersonating legitimate entities. Social engineering techniques manipulate individuals into divulging confidential information or performing actions that could compromise security.

3. Denial of Service (DoS) Attacks: DoS attacks aim to overwhelm a system or network with an excessive amount of traffic, rendering it inaccessible to legitimate users. Distributed Denial of Service (DDoS) attacks amplify the impact by utilizing multiple sources to flood the targeted system.

4. Advanced Persistent Threats (APTs): APTs are sophisticated, long-term cyber-espionage campaigns that target specific organizations or individuals. These attacks involve careful planning, extensive reconnaissance, and persistent efforts to infiltrate and extract sensitive information without detection.

5. Insider Threats: Insider threats arise from individuals within an organization who misuse their access privileges to steal or leak sensitive data. This can occur due to malicious intent, personal gain, or simply negligence.

6. Zero-day Exploits: Zero-day exploits take advantage of vulnerabilities in software that are unknown to the vendor. Attackers exploit these vulnerabilities before a patch or fix is developed, making them a potent weapon in the hands of cybercriminals.

7. Supply Chain Attacks: Supply chain attacks involve compromising the security of a trusted vendor or supplier to gain access to their customers' systems. This tactic allows attackers to bypass traditional security measures and gain a foothold in targeted networks.

8. IoT Vulnerabilities: The proliferation of Internet of Things (IoT) devices has introduced new attack vectors. Inadequate security measures in these devices can allow cybercriminals to gain control over them, potentially leading to data breaches or even physical harm.

Understanding the types of cyber threats and attack vectors is crucial for individuals and organizations to take appropriate measures to protect themselves. By staying informed and implementing robust cybersecurity practices, we can fortify our digital infrastructure, networks, and information against the ever-evolving landscape of cyber threats.

Common Cybersecurity Vulnerabilities

In today's increasingly digital world, where technology permeates every aspect of our lives, cybersecurity has become a critical concern for individuals, organizations, and governments alike. As we continue to rely on digital infrastructure, networks, and information systems, the potential for cyber threats and attacks grows exponentially. It is therefore crucial for teachers, politicians, scholars, academicians, journalists, observers, and diplomats to be aware of the common cybersecurity vulnerabilities that can compromise the security and integrity of our digital ecosystem.

One of the most prevalent cybersecurity vulnerabilities is weak passwords. Many individuals still use easily guessable passwords or reuse the same password across multiple accounts, making it easy for hackers to gain unauthorized access. Educating users about the importance of strong, unique passwords and implementing multi-factor authentication can significantly mitigate this vulnerability.

Another common vulnerability is phishing attacks. Cybercriminals often send fraudulent emails or messages that appear to be from reputable sources, tricking users into revealing sensitive information or clicking on malicious links. Teachers, politicians, scholars, and diplomats should be cautious of such attacks and learn to identify tell-tale signs of phishing attempts to protect themselves and their organizations.

Software vulnerabilities also pose a significant risk. Outdated or unpatched software can contain exploitable flaws that hackers can leverage to gain unauthorized access or launch attacks. Regular software updates and patch management are essential to minimize these vulnerabilities and ensure the security of digital systems.

Insecure network connections are another potential weak point. Public Wi-Fi networks, for example, are often unsecured, exposing users to various risks. It is crucial for teachers, politicians, scholars, and diplomats to be mindful of the network connections they use and consider using virtual private networks (VPNs) to encrypt their online activities and protect sensitive information.

Social engineering is a cybersecurity vulnerability that exploits human psychology. Attackers manipulate individuals through deception, influence, or coercion to obtain confidential information or gain unauthorized access. Awareness training and education can help individuals recognize and resist social engineering techniques, strengthening overall cybersecurity defenses.

Lastly, inadequate cybersecurity measures within organizations can lead to vulnerabilities. Insufficient employee training, lack of robust security protocols, and poor system monitoring can create opportunities for cyber threats. Organizations must prioritize cybersecurity education, implement strong security measures, and regularly assess and update their cybersecurity practices to safeguard their digital assets.

In conclusion, understanding the common cybersecurity vulnerabilities in our digital age is of utmost importance for teachers, politicians, scholars, academicians, journalists, observers, and diplomats. By being aware of these vulnerabilities, individuals can take proactive steps to protect themselves, their organizations, and the digital infrastructure we rely on. Enhanced cybersecurity practices, education, and collaboration are crucial to building a secure and resilient digital ecosystem in the face of evolving cyber threats.

Principles of Secure System Design and Development

In today's digital age, where technology plays a crucial role in every aspect of our lives, ensuring the security of our information has become paramount. As the world becomes increasingly interconnected, the need for robust and secure systems has never been more critical. This subchapter aims to explore the principles of secure system design and development, providing a comprehensive understanding of how to protect digital infrastructure, networks, and information from cyber threats.

The principles of secure system design and development are essential for various stakeholders, including teachers, politicians, scholars, academicians, journalists, observers, and diplomats. As these individuals hold influential positions and deal with sensitive information, it is imperative for them to have a deep understanding of the principles that underpin secure system design and development.

Firstly, a secure system should be built on the principle of defense-in-depth. This means that multiple layers of security mechanisms should be implemented to protect against potential threats. By adopting a layered approach, even if one layer is compromised, other layers will continue to provide protection, mitigating the impact of an attack.

Secondly, secure system design should incorporate the principle of least privilege. This principle ensures that users, processes, and systems are only granted the minimal level of access necessary to perform their tasks effectively. By implementing least privilege, the potential for unauthorized access or misuse of information is significantly reduced.

Another crucial principle is the separation of duties, which aims to prevent a single individual from having complete control over a system or its components. By separating critical tasks, such as system administration, development, and auditing, organizations can reduce the risk of insider threats and ensure accountability.

Additionally, secure system design should prioritize the principle of encryption. Encryption transforms data into a form that can only be understood by authorized parties, providing confidentiality and integrity. By utilizing robust encryption algorithms and key management practices, sensitive information can be protected from unauthorized access and manipulation.

Furthermore, secure system development should adhere to the principle of continuous monitoring and improvement. As cyber threats evolve rapidly, organizations must continuously monitor their systems for vulnerabilities and apply necessary updates and patches in a timely manner. Regular security assessments and audits can help identify potential weaknesses and enable proactive mitigation measures.

In conclusion, the principles of secure system design and development are essential in protecting digital infrastructure, networks, and information from cyber threats. By embracing a defense-in-depth approach, implementing least privilege, separating duties, prioritizing encryption, and embracing continuous monitoring, individuals and organizations can create robust and secure systems. It is imperative for teachers, politicians, scholars, academicians, journalists, observers, and diplomats to understand and apply these principles to ensure the security of their digital assets and maintain the trust of their stakeholders in this increasingly interconnected world.

Chapter 3: Building a Secure Digital Infrastructure

Securing Networks and Communication Systems

In today's digital age, where information flows freely and communication has become seamless, the security of networks and communication systems has become paramount. The rapid advancements in technology have opened up new avenues for cyber threats, making it essential for individuals and organizations to be well-versed in the art of safeguarding their digital infrastructure, networks, and information from potential risks. This subchapter aims to provide teachers, politicians, scholars, academicians, journalists, observers, and diplomats with a comprehensive understanding of the importance of securing networks and communication systems in the realm of cybersecurity.

The subchapter begins by highlighting the escalating frequency and sophistication of cyber threats that target networks and communication systems. It explores the motives behind these attacks, which can range from economic espionage to political sabotage, emphasizing the need for robust security measures. The content delves into the various types of cyber threats faced by individuals and organizations, including malware, phishing attacks, ransomware, and DDoS attacks, among others. It elucidates the potential consequences of a security breach, such as the compromise of sensitive information, financial loss, reputational damage, and even national security implications.

To counter these threats, the subchapter provides an overview of the fundamental principles and best practices for securing networks and communication systems. It discusses the importance of implementing multi-layered security measures, including firewalls, intrusion detection systems, encryption, and user authentication protocols. Additionally, it emphasizes the significance of regular security audits, vulnerability assessments, and incident response plans to ensure the resilience of networks and communication systems.

The content also explores emerging trends and technologies in the field of network and communication system security. It discusses the role of artificial intelligence and machine learning in detecting and mitigating cyber threats, as well as the potential benefits and risks associated with these advancements. Furthermore, it highlights the importance of international cooperation and information sharing in combating cyber threats, underscoring the need for policymakers and diplomats to collaborate on a global scale.

In conclusion, this subchapter serves as a comprehensive guide for teachers, politicians, scholars, academicians, journalists, observers, and diplomats to understand the criticality of securing networks and communication systems in the realm of cybersecurity. By equipping themselves with the knowledge and tools to protect digital infrastructure, networks, and information from cyber threats, individuals and organizations can ensure the integrity, confidentiality, and availability of their data in the digital age.

Protecting Data Centers and Cloud Services

In today's digital age, data centers and cloud services have become the backbone of modern society, facilitating the storage, processing, and transmission of vast amounts of information. However, the increasing reliance on these technologies also opens up new avenues for cyber threats and attacks. This subchapter aims to shed light on the importance of protecting data centers and cloud services and provides insights into effective strategies and best practices.

Data centers, often referred to as the "nerve centers" of an organization, house critical data and applications. Any compromise or breach of these facilities can have severe consequences, including data loss, financial loss, reputational damage, and potential disruptions to essential services. Therefore, it is essential for policymakers, politicians, and diplomats to understand the significance of securing data centers and the cloud.

One of the primary challenges in protecting data centers and cloud services is the constantly evolving nature of cyber threats. Cybercriminals employ sophisticated techniques, such as malware, ransomware, and distributed denial-of-service (DDoS) attacks, to exploit vulnerabilities and gain unauthorized access to sensitive information. As such, a comprehensive approach to cybersecurity is crucial.

This subchapter delves into various aspects of safeguarding data centers and cloud services. It explores the importance of implementing robust security measures, including firewalls, intrusion detection systems, and encryption protocols, to fortify the infrastructure. Additionally, it emphasizes the significance of regular vulnerability assessments and penetration testing to identify and remediate any weaknesses.

Furthermore, the subchapter highlights the role of training and awareness programs for employees and users of data centers and cloud services. Educating individuals about the risks associated with cyber threats, promoting strong password management practices, and fostering a culture of cybersecurity are essential steps in mitigating potential attacks.

Additionally, the subchapter explores the importance of collaboration and information sharing among stakeholders. Policymakers, scholars, and academicians must work hand in hand with cybersecurity experts, journalists, and observers to stay abreast of emerging threats and develop effective countermeasures.

In conclusion, protecting data centers and cloud services is of paramount importance in the digital age. The subchapter provides valuable insights into the challenges faced in safeguarding these critical infrastructures and offers practical recommendations for policymakers, politicians, scholars, academicians, journalists, observers, and diplomats. By implementing robust security measures, fostering a culture of cybersecurity, and promoting collaboration among stakeholders, we can fortify our digital infrastructure and ensure the safe and secure transmission of information in the modern world.

Securing Internet of Things (IoT) Devices

In today's interconnected world, the Internet of Things (IoT) has become an integral part of our daily lives. From smart homes to industrial automation, IoT devices have revolutionized various sectors, improving efficiency and convenience. However, this interconnectedness also introduces new challenges, particularly in terms of cybersecurity. To ensure the continued growth and benefits of the IoT, it is crucial to understand and address the security concerns associated with these devices.

This subchapter aims to provide teachers, politicians, scholars, academicians, journalists, observers, and diplomats with a comprehensive overview of securing IoT devices. It is particularly relevant for those interested in the niche of cybersecurity, focusing on protecting digital infrastructure, networks, and information from cyber threats.

The chapter begins by introducing the concept of IoT and its significance in the digital age. It highlights the various sectors where IoT devices are deployed, such as healthcare, transportation, and smart cities. This sets the stage for understanding the importance of securing these devices to maintain privacy, prevent data breaches, and safeguard critical infrastructure.

Next, the subchapter explores the unique security challenges posed by IoT devices. It delves into the vulnerabilities that can be exploited by cybercriminals, such as weak authentication mechanisms, lack of encryption, and outdated firmware. It also discusses the potential consequences of compromised IoT devices, including unauthorized access to sensitive information, disruption of services, and even physical harm.

To address these challenges, the subchapter provides an overview of best practices and strategies for securing IoT devices. It emphasizes the importance of manufacturers implementing robust security measures from the design phase, including secure communication protocols, regular firmware updates, and encryption. It also highlights the role of users in maintaining device security, such as strong password management, network segmentation, and vigilant monitoring for suspicious activities.

Furthermore, the subchapter delves into the role of policymakers and diplomats in promoting IoT device security. It discusses the need for regulations and standards that encourage manufacturers to prioritize security in their products. It also emphasizes the importance of international cooperation to combat IoT-related cyber threats, as these devices often transcend national boundaries.

By the end of this subchapter, teachers, politicians, scholars, academicians, journalists, observers, and diplomats will have a comprehensive understanding of the security challenges associated with IoT devices and the strategies to mitigate them. They will be equipped with the knowledge required to engage in informed discussions, develop policies, and make decisions that promote a secure and trustworthy IoT ecosystem.

Implementing Secure Software and Hardware

In today's interconnected world, where technology plays a central role in almost every aspect of our lives, the need for secure software and hardware solutions cannot be overstated. With cyber threats evolving at an alarming rate, it is crucial that individuals and organizations take proactive measures to safeguard their digital infrastructure, networks, and sensitive information. This subchapter aims to provide a comprehensive overview of the importance of implementing secure software and hardware, offering valuable insights and practical guidance to teachers, politicians, scholars, academicians, journalists, observers, diplomats, and anyone interested in cybersecurity.

1. Understanding the Threat Landscape: This section will delve into the various cyber threats faced by individuals, organizations, and governments in the digital age. It will explore types of attacks such as malware, ransomware, phishing, and social engineering, shedding light on their potential consequences and the urgency to address them.

2. Secure Software Development: This section will focus on the importance of secure software development practices. It will discuss the need for robust coding standards, vulnerability assessments, and rigorous testing to ensure that software applications are resilient against potential vulnerabilities. The section will also touch upon the significance of regular software updates and patches to address emerging threats.

3. Hardware Security: This section will highlight the critical role of hardware security in protecting digital infrastructure. It will discuss the importance of tamper-proof hardware, secure boot processes, and hardware-based encryption to safeguard against unauthorized access

and data breaches. The section will also explore emerging technologies such as secure enclaves and trusted platform modules.

4. Best Practices for Implementation: This section will provide a practical roadmap for implementing secure software and hardware solutions. It will emphasize the need for collaboration between stakeholders, including developers, policymakers, and end-users, to establish comprehensive security measures. The section will also address the importance of user awareness and training to mitigate human errors and promote a security-focused culture.

5. Ensuring Regulatory Compliance: This section will discuss the role of regulations and standards in promoting the adoption of secure software and hardware practices. It will explore international frameworks and national initiatives aimed at enhancing cybersecurity, emphasizing the need for policymakers to prioritize cybersecurity legislation and enforcement.

By implementing secure software and hardware solutions, individuals, organizations, and governments can significantly reduce the risk of cyber threats and protect their digital assets. This subchapter aims to empower teachers, politicians, scholars, academicians, journalists, observers, and diplomats with the knowledge and tools necessary to navigate the complex landscape of cybersecurity and ensure a safer digital future for all.

Chapter 4: Securing Information and Data

Encryption and Data Protection Techniques

In today's digital age, the security of information has become a paramount concern for individuals and organizations alike. With the rapid growth of technology and the increasing interconnectivity of our world, the need for robust encryption and data protection techniques has never been more critical. This subchapter explores the fundamental concepts and practical applications of encryption and data protection, aiming to equip the audience with an understanding of the tools and strategies necessary to safeguard sensitive information in the face of evolving cyber threats.

Encryption serves as the foundation of modern data protection. It involves the transformation of data into a form that is unreadable by anyone without the corresponding decryption key. Through encryption algorithms, information can be securely transmitted and stored. This subchapter offers an in-depth analysis of various encryption techniques, including symmetric and asymmetric encryption, along with their respective strengths and weaknesses.

Moreover, this subchapter delves into the realm of data protection techniques beyond encryption. It explores additional measures such as access controls, authentication mechanisms, and secure communication protocols. By implementing a multi-layered approach, organizations can significantly enhance the overall security posture of their digital infrastructure, networks, and information.

The content of this subchapter is tailored to meet the needs of teachers, politicians, scholars, academicians, journalists, observers, and diplomats, who are at the forefront of decision-making and policy implementation. It emphasizes the importance of understanding encryption and data protection techniques in the context of cybersecurity. Given the niche audience of cybersecurity, it provides concrete examples and real-world case studies to illustrate the practical implications of encryption and data protection in various sectors, including government, education, finance, and healthcare.

Furthermore, this subchapter addresses the challenges and considerations associated with implementing encryption and data protection techniques. It explores the delicate balance between security and accessibility, highlighting the importance of striking the right equilibrium to ensure the seamless flow of information while maintaining robust protection against cyber threats.

In conclusion, the subchapter "Encryption and Data Protection Techniques" provides a comprehensive overview of the fundamental concepts, practical applications, and challenges associated with securing information in the digital age. It caters to the niche audience of teachers, politicians, scholars, academicians, journalists, observers, and diplomats, who play a pivotal role in shaping policies and strategies to protect digital infrastructure, networks, and information from cyber threats. By equipping the audience with the necessary knowledge and understanding, this subchapter aims to empower them to make informed decisions and contribute to a more secure digital ecosystem.

Access Control and Identity Management

In the digital age, where information flows freely and boundaries between physical and virtual worlds blur, securing sensitive data has become a paramount concern. The subchapter on "Access Control and Identity Management" in our book, "Securing Information in the Digital Age: A Comprehensive Handbook for Politicians and Diplomats," addresses the crucial aspects of protecting digital infrastructure, networks, and information from cyber threats. This chapter is specifically tailored for a diverse audience including teachers, politicians, scholars, academicians, journalists, observers, and diplomats who are keen on understanding the intricacies of cybersecurity.

Access control and identity management are the cornerstones of safeguarding valuable information in the digital realm. This subchapter delves into the fundamental concepts and best practices that enable organizations to control who can access their digital assets and ensure the authenticity of users. It provides a comprehensive overview of the various access control models, such as discretionary, mandatory, and role-based access control, along with their strengths and limitations.

Furthermore, this subchapter explores the significance of identity management in maintaining the integrity of digital systems. It explains the importance of strong authentication mechanisms, including multi-factor authentication, biometrics, and digital certificates, in verifying the identity of users. The chapter also discusses the role of identity and access management (IAM) solutions in streamlining access control processes, enforcing policies, and reducing the risk of unauthorized access.

Drawing on real-world examples and case studies, this subchapter highlights the potential consequences of inadequate access control and identity management. It emphasizes the need for organizations to adopt a proactive approach in implementing robust security measures to mitigate the ever-evolving cyber threats.

Moreover, this subchapter addresses the challenges and ethical considerations associated with access control and identity management. It explores the delicate balance between privacy and security, shedding light on the potential risks of excessive surveillance and the importance of respecting individuals' rights to privacy.

In conclusion, the "Access Control and Identity Management" subchapter of our book is an essential resource for teachers, politicians, scholars, academicians, journalists, observers, and diplomats who are keen on understanding the critical aspects of cybersecurity. By providing a comprehensive overview of access control models, identity management, and associated challenges, this subchapter equips readers with the necessary knowledge to protect digital infrastructure, networks, and information in the digital age.

Data Privacy and Compliance Regulations

In today's digital age, data has become the new currency. From personal information to sensitive business data, the importance of safeguarding this information cannot be overstated. Governments and organizations around the world have recognized the need for robust data privacy and compliance regulations to protect individuals and businesses from cyber threats. This subchapter delves into the intricacies of data privacy and compliance regulations, highlighting their significance and providing insights into their implementation.

Data privacy regulations aim to protect the privacy and confidentiality of personal and sensitive information. These regulations establish guidelines for the collection, storage, processing, and sharing of data, ensuring that individuals have control over their own information. They also define the responsibilities of organizations in maintaining the security and integrity of the data they handle. Compliance with these regulations is crucial to avoid legal and reputational consequences.

The subchapter begins by explaining the fundamental concepts of data privacy and compliance. It explores the importance of data protection and the reasons why compliance regulations are necessary in today's interconnected world. It highlights the potential risks and consequences of data breaches, such as identity theft, financial loss, and reputational damage.

Next, the subchapter delves into the major data privacy and compliance regulations that exist globally. It provides an overview of regulations like the European Union's General Data Protection Regulation (GDPR), the California Consumer Privacy Act (CCPA), and other legislation from different countries. It explores the key principles and provisions of these regulations, emphasizing the rights and responsibilities they establish.

Furthermore, the subchapter discusses the challenges and complexities of implementing data privacy and compliance regulations. It addresses the difficulties faced by organizations in ensuring compliance, especially in a rapidly evolving technological landscape. It also highlights the role of policymakers, educators, and professionals in creating awareness and promoting compliance.

Finally, the subchapter concludes by emphasizing the importance of a comprehensive approach to data privacy and compliance. It stresses the need for continuous education and training to enhance cybersecurity practices and ensure adherence to regulations. It also encourages collaboration between governments, organizations, and individuals to foster a culture of data privacy and compliance.

This subchapter is a valuable resource for teachers, politicians, scholars, academicians, journalists, observers, and diplomats interested in understanding the intricacies of data privacy and compliance regulations. It provides a comprehensive overview of the subject, highlighting its significance in today's digital landscape. By equipping readers with knowledge and insights, it empowers them to make informed decisions and contribute to the protection of data in the digital age.

Incident Response and Data Breach Management

In today's digital age, where technology plays a critical role in every aspect of our lives, the importance of securing information has become paramount. As we rely more and more on digital infrastructure, networks, and information systems, the threat of cyber attacks and data breaches looms large. To effectively combat these threats, it is crucial for teachers, politicians, scholars, academicians, journalists, observers, diplomats, and anyone interested in cybersecurity to understand incident response and data breach management.

The subchapter "Incident Response and Data Breach Management" delves into the essential strategies and practices that organizations and individuals must adopt to effectively respond to cyber incidents and manage data breaches. It provides a comprehensive overview of the steps involved in handling incidents, from detection and containment to eradication and recovery.

First and foremost, the subchapter emphasizes the importance of having an incident response plan in place. This plan serves as a roadmap to guide organizations in the event of a cyber incident, outlining the roles and responsibilities of key stakeholders and establishing a clear chain of command. It emphasizes the need for regular training and simulation exercises to ensure preparedness and effective coordination among teams involved in incident response.

Furthermore, the subchapter highlights the significance of timely detection and containment of cyber incidents. It explores various tools and technologies that organizations can utilize to monitor their networks for any suspicious activities or unauthorized access. It also emphasizes the importance of implementing effective incident response protocols to isolate affected systems and minimize the potential damage.

In the event of a data breach, the subchapter provides insights into the critical steps organizations need to take to manage the breach effectively. It discusses the legal and regulatory obligations surrounding data breaches, including the need to notify affected individuals and regulatory authorities promptly. It also emphasizes the significance of conducting a thorough forensic investigation to identify the root cause of the breach and prevent future incidents.

Overall, "Incident Response and Data Breach Management" is a vital subchapter in the book "Securing Information in the Digital Age: A Comprehensive Handbook for Politicians and Diplomats." It equips teachers, politicians, scholars, academicians, journalists, observers, diplomats, and anyone interested in cybersecurity with the knowledge and tools necessary to respond swiftly and effectively to cyber incidents and manage data breaches. By understanding and implementing the strategies outlined in this subchapter, individuals and organizations can better protect their digital infrastructure, networks, and valuable information from the ever-evolving cyber threats of the modern world.

Chapter 5: Cybersecurity Governance and Policy

National Cybersecurity Strategies and Frameworks

In today's digitally interconnected world, the need for robust cybersecurity measures has become paramount. As the threat landscape continues to evolve, nations are recognizing the importance of developing comprehensive national cybersecurity strategies and frameworks to safeguard their digital infrastructure, networks, and information from cyber threats. This subchapter explores the key elements and considerations in crafting effective national cybersecurity strategies and frameworks.

1. Understanding the Cyber Threat Landscape:

To develop a successful cybersecurity strategy, policymakers and decision-makers must first comprehend the evolving cyber threat landscape. This includes understanding the various types of cyber threats, such as malware, phishing attacks, and advanced persistent threats (APTs). Additionally, policymakers need to be aware of emerging trends, including the increasing sophistication of cybercriminals and state-sponsored cyber espionage.

2. Developing a National Cybersecurity Framework:

A national cybersecurity framework serves as a blueprint for guiding a country's cybersecurity efforts. It outlines the overarching goals, principles, and strategies to be employed. This framework should be adaptable to changing technologies and threat landscapes. Additionally, it should consider international best practices and standards, such as those provided by organizations like the

International Organization for Standardization (ISO) and the National Institute of Standards and Technology (NIST).

3. Collaboration and Public-Private Partnerships:

Effective cybersecurity strategies require collaboration among various stakeholders, including government agencies, private sector entities, academia, and civil society. Policymakers should foster public-private partnerships to share information, resources, and expertise. Collaboration enhances situational awareness, enables the development of robust defense mechanisms, and facilitates the exchange of best practices.

4. Capacity Building and Education:

Developing a cybersecurity-savvy workforce is critical to tackling cyber threats effectively. Governments must invest in capacity building programs to train cybersecurity professionals and raise awareness among all citizens. Policymakers should promote cybersecurity education at all levels, from schools to universities, and provide specialized training for law enforcement agencies to combat cybercrime effectively.

5. Incident Response and Recovery:

No cybersecurity strategy can be complete without an effective incident response and recovery plan. Governments must establish dedicated cyber incident response teams and establish protocols for reporting, analyzing, and mitigating cyber incidents. Rapid response and recovery are essential to minimizing the impact of cyberattacks and restoring critical services.

6. Continuous Evaluation and Adaptation:

Cyber threats are constantly evolving, and national cybersecurity strategies must keep pace. Regular evaluation of the strategy's effectiveness is crucial. Governments need to establish mechanisms for monitoring, assessing, and updating their cybersecurity frameworks to address emerging threats effectively.

In conclusion, the development of national cybersecurity strategies and frameworks is paramount for protecting digital infrastructure, networks, and information from cyber threats. By understanding the cyber threat landscape, fostering collaboration, investing in capacity building, establishing incident response mechanisms, and continuously evaluating and adapting their strategies, nations can enhance their cybersecurity posture. Policymakers, educators, scholars, and diplomats must work together to ensure the success of these strategies and promote a safe and secure digital age for all.

International Cooperation and Cybersecurity Diplomacy

In today's interconnected world, where digital technologies have become an integral part of our daily lives, the need for robust cybersecurity measures cannot be overstated. Cyber threats, ranging from data breaches to ransomware attacks, have the potential to disrupt economies, compromise national security, and violate individual privacy. Addressing these challenges requires a collaborative effort on a global scale, making international cooperation and cybersecurity diplomacy crucial.

The subchapter on "International Cooperation and Cybersecurity Diplomacy" in the book "Securing Information in the Digital Age: A Comprehensive Handbook for Politicians and Diplomats" aims to provide a comprehensive understanding of the significance of international collaboration in safeguarding digital infrastructure, networks, and information from cyber threats.

For teachers, politicians, scholars, academicians, journalists, observers, and diplomats interested in the field of cybersecurity, this subchapter serves as a valuable resource. It sheds light on the importance of diplomacy in fostering dialogue, building trust, and developing common norms and rules to address cyber threats effectively.

The subchapter begins by exploring the current landscape of cyber threats and their potential impact on various sectors, including finance, healthcare, government, and critical infrastructure. It highlights the increasing sophistication of cyber attacks and the need for a coordinated response to counter these evolving threats.

Drawing on real-world examples, the subchapter delves into the role of international organizations, such as the United Nations, NATO, and the European Union, in promoting cybersecurity cooperation among nations. It examines the initiatives, agreements, and frameworks that have been developed to facilitate information sharing, capacity building, and joint response mechanisms.

Furthermore, the subchapter discusses the challenges and barriers to international cooperation in cybersecurity, including differing national interests, legal frameworks, and cultural norms. It analyzes case studies of successful and unsuccessful collaborative efforts, providing valuable insights into the factors that contribute to effective cybersecurity diplomacy.

The subchapter concludes by emphasizing the need for ongoing engagement and dialogue among nations, highlighting the importance of trust-building measures, information exchange, and joint exercises. It stresses the role of diplomats in bridging the gap between technical experts, policymakers, and other stakeholders, facilitating meaningful discussions and negotiations.

Overall, "International Cooperation and Cybersecurity Diplomacy" serves as a comprehensive guide for individuals interested in the niche of cybersecurity. It provides a nuanced understanding of the challenges and opportunities in the realm of international cybersecurity cooperation, empowering policymakers, scholars, and diplomats with the knowledge and tools necessary to navigate the complex landscape of digital security.

Public-Private Partnerships in Cybersecurity

In today's digital age, the threat landscape has evolved exponentially, with cyber attacks becoming more sophisticated and frequent. As nations and organizations grapple with the challenges posed by these threats, the concept of public-private partnerships has emerged as a vital strategy in ensuring the robust protection of digital infrastructure, networks, and information.

This subchapter delves into the significance of public-private partnerships in cybersecurity, highlighting the roles of various stakeholders in addressing cyber threats. Aimed at teachers, politicians, scholars, academicians, journalists, observers, and diplomats, this section provides a comprehensive understanding of the collaborative efforts required to safeguard our digital ecosystem.

The importance of public-private partnerships cannot be overstated, as they bring together the expertise, resources, and perspectives of both the public and private sectors. Governments possess the regulatory power, intelligence capabilities, and legal framework necessary to combat cyber threats effectively. On the other hand, private organizations, including technology giants, financial institutions, and critical infrastructure providers, play a crucial role in developing innovative cybersecurity solutions and implementing best practices.

This subchapter explores successful examples of public-private partnerships in cybersecurity, showcasing initiatives such as information sharing platforms, joint research projects, and collaborative incident response mechanisms. It emphasizes the need for open communication channels between governments and private entities to exchange threat intelligence and coordinate response efforts swiftly.

Moreover, this section sheds light on the challenges faced by public-private partnerships in cybersecurity. Issues such as information asymmetry, legal and regulatory hurdles, and divergent priorities are examined, along with strategies to overcome these obstacles. It underscores the significance of trust-building measures and the necessity of aligning interests to ensure fruitful collaboration.

Furthermore, this subchapter provides insights into the evolving nature of cyber threats and the need for continuous adaptation in public-private partnerships. It discusses the importance of fostering a culture of cybersecurity awareness among all stakeholders and the role of education and training programs in promoting cyber resilience.

By the end of this subchapter, teachers, politicians, scholars, academicians, journalists, observers, and diplomats will have a deep understanding of the crucial role public-private partnerships play in cybersecurity. They will be equipped with the knowledge to advocate for and contribute to the development of effective collaborations that protect our digital infrastructure, networks, and information from the ever-evolving cyber threats of the digital age.

Legislation and Regulations for Cybersecurity

In today's digital age, the rapid advancement of technology has brought countless benefits to our lives. However, it has also opened the door to new and sophisticated cyber threats that can compromise our digital infrastructure, networks, and information. To address these challenges, robust legislation and regulations for cybersecurity are crucial to safeguarding our digital landscape.

This subchapter delves into the importance of legislation and regulations in the realm of cybersecurity. It aims to provide teachers, politicians, scholars, academicians, journalists, observers, and diplomats with a comprehensive understanding of the role they play in protecting our digital assets.

To begin with, legislation serves as a foundation for creating a legal framework to combat cyber threats. It provides authorities with the necessary tools to investigate, prosecute, and punish cybercriminals. By defining cybercrimes and specifying penalties, legislation acts as a deterrent, discouraging potential offenders from engaging in malicious activities.

Furthermore, regulations play a vital role in implementing legislation effectively. They provide guidelines and standards that organizations and individuals must adhere to, ensuring a consistent and unified approach to cybersecurity. Regulations also encourage the adoption of best practices, promoting a culture of security and resilience across sectors.

In this subchapter, we explore various legislative and regulatory measures that have been implemented globally. We examine how different countries have addressed the challenges posed by cyber threats and discuss the lessons we can learn from their experiences.

Moreover, we shed light on international cooperation and collaboration in the field of cybersecurity. Given the borderless nature of cyber threats, effective legislation and regulations should extend beyond national boundaries. We discuss the importance of international agreements and initiatives in fostering information sharing, capacity building, and joint response mechanisms.

Lastly, we delve into the evolving landscape of cybersecurity and the need for continuous updates to legislation and regulations. As technology advances and new threats emerge, it is essential to adapt our legal frameworks accordingly. We explore the challenges faced in keeping pace with the ever-changing cyber landscape and propose strategies to mitigate them.

Overall, this subchapter aims to equip teachers, politicians, scholars, academicians, journalists, observers, and diplomats with the knowledge and insights necessary to understand, advocate for, and shape legislation and regulations for cybersecurity. By doing so, we can collectively work towards securing our digital age and safeguarding the interests of individuals, organizations, and nations.

Chapter 6: Cyber Threat Intelligence and Defense

Cyber Threat Intelligence Gathering and Analysis

In today's interconnected digital landscape, the need for robust cybersecurity measures has become paramount. As technology evolves, so do the tactics employed by cybercriminals, making it crucial for individuals and organizations to stay one step ahead. This subchapter, "Cyber Threat Intelligence Gathering and Analysis," delves into the intricacies of gathering and analyzing cyber threat intelligence, equipping teachers, politicians, scholars, academicians, journalists, observers, diplomats, and anyone interested in cybersecurity with valuable insights.

The subchapter begins by outlining the importance of cyber threat intelligence as a proactive approach to identifying and mitigating cyber risks. It emphasizes the significance of real-time information, which enables stakeholders to make informed decisions, develop effective strategies, and respond promptly to emerging threats. By empowering individuals and organizations with actionable intelligence, cyber threat intelligence plays a pivotal role in safeguarding digital infrastructure, networks, and critical information.

Next, the subchapter explores the various sources and methods used for gathering cyber threat intelligence. It delves into open-source intelligence, dark web monitoring, social media analysis, honeypots, and collaboration with industry peers and government agencies. By understanding the strengths and limitations of each source, readers will gain a comprehensive overview of the intelligence gathering landscape.

Furthermore, the subchapter provides an in-depth analysis of the techniques employed in analyzing cyber threat intelligence. It highlights the importance of contextualizing information and extracting meaningful insights. It introduces concepts such as indicator of compromise (IOC) analysis, behavioral analysis, and threat modeling to help readers effectively assess the severity and potential impact of cyber threats.

Moreover, the subchapter explores the role of machine learning, artificial intelligence, and big data analytics in cyber threat intelligence gathering and analysis. It discusses how these technologies can enhance the speed and accuracy of threat detection and prediction. It also addresses the ethical considerations associated with the use of these technologies, emphasizing the need for responsible and transparent practices.

In conclusion, "Cyber Threat Intelligence Gathering and Analysis" is a comprehensive subchapter that equips teachers, politicians, scholars, academicians, journalists, observers, and diplomats with the knowledge and tools necessary to navigate the complex world of cyber threats. By understanding the importance of proactive intelligence gathering and effective analysis, readers will be better equipped to protect digital infrastructure, networks, and information from cyber threats.

Detecting and Responding to Cyber Attacks

In today's increasingly interconnected and digital world, the threat of cyber attacks looms large over individuals, organizations, and even nations. The rapid advancement of technology has opened up new avenues for both malicious actors and state-sponsored entities to exploit vulnerabilities in digital infrastructure, networks, and information. As such, it is imperative for individuals and institutions to be proactive in detecting and responding to these cyber threats.

This subchapter, "Detecting and Responding to Cyber Attacks," is a crucial resource that aims to equip teachers, politicians, scholars, academicians, journalists, observers, and diplomats with the knowledge and tools necessary to understand and combat cyber attacks effectively. It provides a comprehensive overview of the techniques and strategies employed in detecting and responding to these threats, ensuring the security and integrity of digital assets.

The subchapter begins by delving into the intricacies of cyber attacks, outlining the various types and motivations behind them. It explores the methods employed by hackers, such as phishing, malware, and ransomware, and the potential consequences of successful cyber attacks on individuals, organizations, and even national security. By understanding the nature of these threats, readers can grasp the urgency and importance of adopting robust cybersecurity measures.

The content then delves into the crucial aspect of detecting cyber attacks. It explores the use of advanced monitoring systems, intrusion detection software, and threat intelligence to identify potential vulnerabilities and breaches in digital infrastructure. Moreover, it emphasizes the significance of continuous monitoring and analysis of network traffic, system logs, and user behavior to detect any suspicious activities promptly.

Once a cyber attack is detected, the subchapter provides a comprehensive guide on responding effectively to mitigate the damage and prevent further infiltration. It outlines the steps to be taken, including isolating affected systems, conducting forensic investigations, and implementing incident response plans. It also highlights the importance of collaboration and information sharing between different stakeholders, such as government agencies, private sector entities, and cybersecurity experts, to ensure a coordinated response and swift recovery.

By the end of this subchapter, teachers, politicians, scholars, academicians, journalists, observers, and diplomats will have gained a deeper understanding of the evolving cyber threat landscape and the strategies to detect and respond to cyber attacks effectively. Armed with this knowledge, they can play a crucial role in advocating for robust cybersecurity policies, implementing preventive measures, and fostering international cooperation to combat cyber threats and safeguard digital infrastructure, networks, and information.

Cybersecurity Best Practices and Defensive Techniques

In today's digital age, where technology has become an integral part of our lives, the need for robust cybersecurity measures is more critical than ever. With the constant evolution of cyber threats, it is imperative that individuals and organizations implement best practices and defensive techniques to protect their digital infrastructure, networks, and sensitive information. This subchapter aims to provide teachers, politicians, scholars, academicians, journalists, observers, and diplomats with a comprehensive understanding of cybersecurity best practices and defensive techniques.

First and foremost, staying informed about the latest cyber threats and vulnerabilities is crucial. Teachers can educate their students about the risks associated with online activities, while politicians and diplomats can advocate for policies that promote cybersecurity awareness and education. Scholars and academicians can conduct research that advances our understanding of cyber threats, and journalists and observers can disseminate information to the public about recent cyber attacks and their implications.

Implementing strong passwords and regularly updating them is another fundamental aspect of cybersecurity. This applies to all individuals, regardless of their professional background. By using complex and unique passwords for each online account, teachers, politicians, scholars, and others can significantly reduce the risk of unauthorized access. Furthermore, enabling two-factor authentication adds an extra layer of security, making it harder for cybercriminals to compromise accounts.

Data encryption and secure communication protocols are also critical in safeguarding sensitive information. Teachers can ensure that their students are aware of encryption techniques and the importance of using secure channels when transmitting confidential data. Politicians and diplomats should prioritize the use of encrypted communication platforms to protect sensitive discussions and negotiations. Scholars and academicians can contribute to the development of new encryption algorithms and methodologies, while journalists and observers can promote the use of secure communication tools for whistleblowers and journalists reporting on sensitive topics.

Regularly updating software and applying security patches is essential to prevent cyber attacks. Teachers should instruct their students on the importance of updating their devices and software to ensure they have the latest security features. Politicians and diplomats should enforce policies that mandate regular updates and patch management. Scholars and academicians can contribute to the development of secure software systems, while journalists and observers can raise awareness about the risks of using outdated software.

In conclusion, cybersecurity best practices and defensive techniques are vital in protecting digital infrastructure, networks, and information from cyber threats. Teachers, politicians, scholars, academicians, journalists, observers, and diplomats all play a crucial role in implementing and promoting these practices. By staying informed, using strong passwords, encrypting data, updating software, and following other cybersecurity best practices, we can create a safer digital environment for everyone.

Cybersecurity Awareness and Training Programs

In an increasingly interconnected world, where digital infrastructure, networks, and information are vulnerable to a plethora of cyber threats, it has become crucial for individuals and organizations to prioritize cybersecurity awareness and training programs. These programs play a pivotal role in equipping teachers, politicians, scholars, academicians, journalists, observers, and diplomats with the knowledge and skills necessary to protect themselves and their institutions from cyber attacks.

Cybersecurity, with its multifaceted dimensions, requires a comprehensive approach that encompasses both technical understanding and awareness of the human element involved in digital security. Cybersecurity awareness programs aim to educate individuals about the potential risks and vulnerabilities associated with operating in the digital realm. By raising awareness about common cyber threats, such as phishing attempts, malware, and social engineering, these programs empower individuals to make informed decisions and adopt secure practices in their digital interactions.

Moreover, cybersecurity training programs are designed to provide individuals with the skills and expertise required to safeguard digital infrastructure and networks. These programs equip participants with the knowledge of industry best practices, incident response strategies, and the implementation of robust security measures. By engaging in hands-on training exercises and simulations, participants gain practical experience in detecting, preventing, and mitigating cyber threats.

For teachers, cybersecurity awareness and training programs enable them to educate the younger generation about safe online practices. By integrating cybersecurity education into the curriculum, teachers can instill responsible digital behavior among students, ensuring they are equipped to navigate the digital landscape securely. This, in turn, creates a cyber-literate generation that can contribute to a safer digital future.

Politicians and diplomats also benefit greatly from cybersecurity awareness and training programs. As decision-makers and representatives of their nations, they must understand the potential implications of cyber attacks on critical infrastructure and national security. By undergoing cybersecurity training, politicians and diplomats can better comprehend the complexities of cyber threats, enabling them to make informed policy decisions and implement effective cybersecurity measures.

Scholars, academicians, journalists, observers, and diplomats, who often handle sensitive information, are also prime targets for cyber attacks. Cybersecurity awareness and training programs provide them with the necessary knowledge and tools to protect their research, sources, and communications. By understanding the ever-evolving threat landscape, they can adopt proactive measures to safeguard their work and preserve the integrity of their information.

In conclusion, cybersecurity awareness and training programs are indispensable in today's digital age. These programs equip teachers, politicians, scholars, academicians, journalists, observers, and diplomats with the knowledge and skills needed to navigate the digital landscape securely. By fostering a cyber-literate society and organizations, we can collectively work towards safeguarding our digital infrastructure, networks, and information from cyber threats.

Chapter 7: Emerging Trends and Future Challenges

Artificial Intelligence and Machine Learning in Cybersecurity

In the digital age, the rapid advancements in technology have brought about countless benefits, but they have also given rise to new challenges and threats. One of the most pressing concerns today is cybersecurity, which focuses on protecting digital infrastructure, networks, and information from cyber threats. As these threats continue to evolve and become more sophisticated, traditional security measures alone are no longer sufficient. This is where the power of Artificial Intelligence (AI) and Machine Learning (ML) comes into play.

AI and ML have revolutionized various industries, and their application in cybersecurity has proven to be a game-changer. By utilizing AI and ML algorithms, cybersecurity professionals are now better equipped to detect, prevent, and respond to cyber threats in real-time. These technologies can analyze massive amounts of data, identify patterns, and learn from past incidents to predict and mitigate future attacks.

This subchapter explores the potential of AI and ML in the field of cybersecurity, offering insights and strategies for teachers, politicians, scholars, academicians, journalists, observers, and diplomats to effectively navigate this complex landscape.

First and foremost, it delves into the capabilities of AI and ML in threat detection and prevention. These technologies can analyze vast amounts of network traffic, identify anomalies, and pinpoint potential vulnerabilities. By continuously monitoring and analyzing data, AI and ML can rapidly identify new threat vectors and generate proactive defense mechanisms.

Furthermore, the subchapter discusses the role of AI and ML in incident response and mitigation. When a cyber attack occurs, time is of the essence. AI and ML algorithms can swiftly analyze the attack, determine its severity, and suggest appropriate countermeasures. This can significantly reduce response time, minimize the impact of the attack, and enable rapid recovery.

However, it is essential to address the ethical considerations associated with the use of AI and ML in cybersecurity. The subchapter explores the potential risks and challenges, such as algorithmic bias, privacy concerns, and unintended consequences. It emphasizes the need for responsible and transparent use of these technologies, ensuring that they do not infringe upon individual rights or perpetuate discrimination.

In conclusion, the integration of AI and ML in cybersecurity is transforming the way we protect our digital infrastructure and information. This subchapter provides valuable insights for teachers, politicians, scholars, academicians, journalists, observers, and diplomats, enabling them to understand and harness the power of AI and ML in safeguarding our digital age. By embracing these technologies responsibly, we can stay one step ahead of cyber threats and ensure a secure digital future for all.

Securing Critical Infrastructures

In today's digitally dependent world, the security of critical infrastructures has become a paramount concern. From power grids and transportation systems to financial institutions and healthcare facilities, these infrastructures play a vital role in our everyday lives. However, they are increasingly vulnerable to cyber threats that can disrupt their operations, compromise sensitive information, and even put lives at risk. Therefore, it is imperative for policymakers, diplomats, and scholars to understand the challenges and strategies involved in securing these critical systems.

The chapter "Securing Critical Infrastructures" aims to provide a comprehensive overview of the measures necessary to protect vital infrastructures from cyber threats. Targeted towards teachers, politicians, scholars, academicians, journalists, observers, and diplomats, it offers valuable insights into the world of cybersecurity and its significance in safeguarding digital infrastructure, networks, and information.

The subchapter begins by exploring the various types of critical infrastructures and the unique challenges they face in the digital age. It examines the interconnectivity of these systems and the potential consequences of a cyber attack, underscoring the need for a proactive approach to cybersecurity.

Next, the chapter delves into the current threat landscape, shedding light on the evolving tactics employed by malicious actors. It emphasizes the importance of understanding the motives behind cyber attacks and the potential impact they can have on national security, economic stability, and public trust.

The subchapter then moves on to discuss the key principles and strategies for securing critical infrastructures. It explores the concept of resilience, emphasizing the need for redundancy, rapid response capabilities, and effective incident management. It also highlights the importance of collaboration between government agencies, private sector entities, and international partners to enhance information sharing and coordinate response efforts.

Furthermore, the subchapter delves into the role of emerging technologies, such as artificial intelligence and blockchain, in bolstering the security of critical infrastructures. It explores their potential benefits and challenges, offering insights into their implementation and integration into existing systems.

In conclusion, "Securing Critical Infrastructures" serves as an essential guide for policymakers, diplomats, and scholars seeking to understand and address the cybersecurity challenges faced by critical infrastructures. By adopting a proactive approach, implementing robust security measures, and fostering collaboration, we can ensure the resilience and integrity of these vital systems in the digital age.

Internet Governance and Cybersecurity

Introduction

In today's interconnected world, the internet plays a central role in our daily lives, revolutionizing communication, commerce, and information sharing. However, with this immense power comes great responsibility. The subchapter on "Internet Governance and Cybersecurity" in the book "Securing Information in the Digital Age: A Comprehensive Handbook for Politicians and Diplomats" addresses the pressing need for effective governance and robust cybersecurity measures in the digital realm. Aimed at teachers, politicians, scholars, academicians, journalists, observers, and diplomats, this subchapter provides a comprehensive overview of the challenges and strategies in safeguarding digital infrastructure, networks, and information from cyber threats.

Understanding Internet Governance

Internet governance refers to the mechanisms, policies, and processes that shape and regulate the development and use of the internet. It encompasses a wide range of issues, including access, infrastructure, content regulation, privacy, and cybersecurity. The subchapter explores the complex landscape of internet governance, highlighting the roles and responsibilities of various stakeholders, such as governments, international organizations, civil society, and the private sector.

Importance of Cybersecurity

Cybersecurity is a critical component of internet governance, focusing on protecting digital infrastructure, networks, and information from cyber threats. As technology advances, so do the techniques employed by cybercriminals and state-sponsored actors. The subchapter delves into the evolving nature of cyber threats and their potential impact on various sectors, including finance, healthcare, critical infrastructure, and national security.

Strategies for Effective Cybersecurity

To combat the ever-growing cyber threats, the subchapter presents a range of strategies for effective cybersecurity. These include:

1. International Cooperation: Given the transnational nature of cyber threats, collaboration and information sharing among nations are crucial. The subchapter emphasizes the need for international agreements, norms, and frameworks to foster cooperation in combating cybercrime and enhancing cybersecurity.

2. Capacity Building: As cyber threats become more sophisticated, individuals and organizations must develop the necessary skills and expertise to protect themselves. The subchapter explores the importance of capacity building initiatives, such as training programs, educational campaigns, and awareness-raising efforts.

3. Robust Legal Frameworks: A comprehensive legal framework is essential to deter cybercriminals and ensure accountability. The subchapter examines the existing legal mechanisms and highlights the need for harmonization and updates to address emerging challenges.

4. Public-Private Partnerships: Cybersecurity cannot be achieved by governments alone. The subchapter emphasizes the significance of collaboration between the public and private sectors to share resources, expertise, and best practices.

Conclusion

In conclusion, the subchapter on "Internet Governance and Cybersecurity" provides a comprehensive and informative guide to the challenges and strategies surrounding the protection of digital infrastructure, networks, and information from cyber threats. Aimed at teachers, politicians, scholars, academicians, journalists, observers, and diplomats, this subchapter serves as a valuable resource for understanding the complexities of internet governance and the importance of robust cybersecurity measures. By adopting the strategies outlined in this subchapter, stakeholders can work together to safeguard the digital age and ensure a secure and resilient cyberspace for all.

Ethical Considerations in Cybersecurity

In today's digital age, where technology plays a pivotal role in our lives, the importance of cybersecurity cannot be overstated. As we increasingly rely on digital infrastructure, networks, and information systems, the need to protect them from cyber threats becomes paramount. However, the pursuit of robust cybersecurity measures raises several ethical considerations that demand careful attention and deliberation.

This subchapter aims to address the ethical dimensions of cybersecurity and shed light on the complex issues that arise in this domain. It is intended for teachers, politicians, scholars, academicians, journalists, observers, and diplomats who are interested in understanding and navigating the ethical challenges associated with cybersecurity.

One of the most significant ethical considerations in cybersecurity is the balance between privacy and security. While it is crucial to protect sensitive information and prevent cyberattacks, it is equally important to respect individuals' rights to privacy. Striking the right balance between these two values requires thoughtful deliberation and the implementation of privacy-enhancing technologies and policies.

Another ethical concern in cybersecurity relates to the potential for discrimination and bias. As cybersecurity measures are designed and implemented, there is a risk of disproportionately impacting certain groups or communities. For instance, the deployment of surveillance technologies may inadvertently target specific ethnic or religious groups, leading to discrimination and violation of human rights. Policymakers and practitioners need to be mindful of these risks and ensure that cybersecurity measures are fair, transparent, and inclusive.

Furthermore, the ethical implications of offensive cybersecurity strategies cannot be ignored. While offensive tactics may be employed to protect national interests or preemptively defend against cyber threats, they raise questions about the line between defense and aggression. The use of offensive cyber capabilities should be carefully regulated to prevent unintended consequences and minimize the potential for escalating conflicts.

Lastly, the global nature of cybersecurity necessitates international cooperation and collaboration. Ethical considerations in cybersecurity extend to international relations, diplomacy, and the development of norms and regulations. Building consensus on ethical guidelines and fostering international cooperation in addressing cyber threats is essential to ensure a secure and ethical digital environment.

In conclusion, the field of cybersecurity presents numerous ethical challenges that demand our attention and deliberation. Balancing privacy and security, addressing discrimination and bias, regulating offensive cyber strategies, and fostering international cooperation are all crucial aspects of ethical considerations in cybersecurity. By engaging in thoughtful discussions and implementing ethical frameworks, we can navigate these challenges and strive for a secure and ethical digital age.

Chapter 8: Case Studies and Real-World Examples

Notable Cyber Attacks and Their Impacts

In the digital age, the world is increasingly interconnected and reliant on information technology. However, this dependence comes with a significant vulnerability - the threat of cyber attacks. Cybersecurity plays a crucial role in protecting our digital infrastructure, networks, and information from malicious actors. It is imperative for teachers, politicians, scholars, academicians, journalists, observers, and diplomats to understand the notable cyber attacks that have occurred and the profound impacts they have had on society.

One such notable cyber attack was the Stuxnet worm, discovered in 2010. Stuxnet was a highly sophisticated malware that specifically targeted Iran's nuclear program. It infiltrated the computer systems controlling centrifuges used in uranium enrichment, causing them to malfunction and disrupting Iran's nuclear ambitions. This attack demonstrated the potential for cyber weapons to cause physical damage, highlighting the need for robust cybersecurity measures to protect critical infrastructure.

Another significant cyber attack was the 2014 breach of the U.S. Office of Personnel Management (OPM). This breach exposed highly sensitive personal information of more than 22 million current and former government employees, including security clearance details. The impact of this attack was far-reaching, compromising national security and exposing individuals to potential identity theft and espionage. It underscored the importance of safeguarding sensitive government data and the need for strong cybersecurity practices in all sectors.

The WannaCry ransomware attack in 2017 was particularly devastating. This global attack affected hundreds of thousands of computers in over 150 countries, encrypting files and demanding ransom payments in Bitcoin. The attack targeted vulnerabilities in outdated software, highlighting the need for regular updates and patches to prevent such incidents. The widespread disruption caused by WannaCry emphasized the interconnectedness of the digital world and the need for collaborative efforts to combat cyber threats.

These notable cyber attacks and their impacts serve as a wake-up call for all stakeholders. Teachers can educate students on the importance of cybersecurity and instill responsible digital practices. Politicians must enact legislation and policies that prioritize cybersecurity as a national security concern. Scholars and academicians can conduct research to develop innovative technologies and strategies to counter evolving cyber threats. Journalists and observers play a vital role in raising awareness and holding governments and organizations accountable for cybersecurity lapses. Finally, diplomats must engage in international cooperation to establish norms and protocols to prevent and respond to cyber attacks.

In conclusion, understanding the notable cyber attacks and their impacts is crucial in addressing the challenges posed by cyber threats. By acknowledging the vulnerabilities and learning from past incidents, we can collectively work towards securing information in the digital age and protecting our digital infrastructure, networks, and information from cyber threats.

Successful Cybersecurity Implementations

In an increasingly digital world, the need for robust cybersecurity measures is paramount. In this subchapter, we will explore successful cybersecurity implementations that have proven effective in protecting digital infrastructure, networks, and information from cyber threats.

This comprehensive handbook is specifically addressed to teachers, politicians, scholars, academicians, journalists, observers, and diplomats who are involved in the field of cybersecurity.

The rapid advancement of technology presents both opportunities and challenges. While it has empowered individuals and organizations, it has also given rise to sophisticated cyber threats. Therefore, understanding and implementing effective cybersecurity strategies is crucial to safeguarding our digital assets.

One key aspect of successful cybersecurity implementation is adopting a multi-layered approach. This involves utilizing a combination of technical controls, policies, and procedures to create multiple barriers against potential threats. It encompasses aspects such as network security, endpoint protection, data encryption, access controls, and incident response plans.

Furthermore, successful cybersecurity implementations require a proactive stance rather than a reactive one. Organizations must stay vigilant and continuously update their security systems to address emerging threats. This necessitates regular risk assessments, vulnerability scans, and penetration testing to identify and patch potential weaknesses.

Another vital component of successful cybersecurity implementations is fostering a culture of cybersecurity awareness. Educating and training employees, end-users, and stakeholders about potential risks and best practices is paramount. This includes teaching them about the importance of strong passwords, data privacy, social engineering, and recognizing phishing attempts.

Collaboration and information sharing also play a significant role in successful cybersecurity implementations. Governments, organizations, and individuals must work together to exchange threat intelligence, best practices, and lessons learned. This includes partnerships between public and private sectors, international cooperation, and participation in cybersecurity conferences, workshops, and forums.

Moreover, successful cybersecurity implementations require robust legal frameworks and policies. Policymakers and diplomats must advocate for legislation that enforces accountability, data protection, and international cooperation in combating cyber threats. This involves addressing issues such as cybercrime, data breaches, intellectual property theft, and cyber espionage.

In conclusion, successful cybersecurity implementations are essential in safeguarding our digital infrastructure, networks, and information from cyber threats. By adopting a multi-layered approach, proactive measures, fostering cybersecurity awareness, promoting collaboration, and implementing robust legal frameworks, we can mitigate risks and protect our digital assets. This comprehensive handbook aims to equip teachers, politicians, scholars, academicians, journalists, observers, and diplomats with the necessary knowledge and tools to navigate the complex world of cybersecurity.

Lessons Learned from Cybersecurity Incidents

In this rapidly evolving digital age, the importance of cybersecurity cannot be overstated. With the increasing sophistication of cyber threats and the potential for devastating consequences, it is crucial for individuals and organizations to learn from past cybersecurity incidents. This subchapter aims to provide valuable insights and lessons learned, serving as a comprehensive guide for educators, politicians, scholars, academicians, journalists, observers, and diplomats involved in the field of cybersecurity.

1. The Threat Landscape: Understanding the ever-changing threat landscape is vital. Cybersecurity incidents highlight the need for continuous monitoring and staying updated on emerging threats, vulnerabilities, and attack techniques. By recognizing the tactics employed by cybercriminals, policymakers and educators can effectively develop robust strategies and educational programs to mitigate risks.

2. Importance of Collaboration: Cybersecurity incidents have emphasized the importance of collaboration among all stakeholders. Governments, private organizations, academia, and individuals must work together to build a resilient digital ecosystem. Sharing information, best practices, and threat intelligence can significantly enhance the collective defense against cyber threats.

3. Proactive Defense: Reactive approaches to cybersecurity are insufficient. Incidents have shown that organizations and individuals must adopt a proactive mindset, investing in preventive measures such as regular security assessments, vulnerability scanning, and employee training. By taking a proactive stance, potential cyber threats can be detected and mitigated before they cause significant harm.

4. Public Awareness and Education: Educating the public about cybersecurity risks and best practices is paramount. Governments, schools, and media play a crucial role in raising awareness among citizens. By integrating cybersecurity education into curricula, policymakers can empower the younger generation to navigate the digital world safely and responsibly.

5. Cyber Diplomacy: Cybersecurity incidents transcend national borders, necessitating international cooperation. Diplomats and policymakers must prioritize cyber diplomacy to foster trust and collaboration among nations. Establishing cyber norms,

information-sharing agreements, and joint cybersecurity exercises are essential steps in mitigating global cyber threats.

6. Resilience and Incident Response: The ability to respond swiftly and effectively to cyber incidents is critical. Organizations should establish robust incident response plans, conduct regular drills, and invest in resilient infrastructure. By learning from past incidents, policymakers can develop comprehensive frameworks that enable quick recovery and minimize damage.

In conclusion, the lessons learned from cybersecurity incidents play a vital role in shaping policies, practices, and education in the digital age. By implementing proactive defense strategies, fostering collaboration, raising public awareness, prioritizing cyber diplomacy, and enhancing incident response capabilities, individuals and organizations can better protect digital infrastructure, networks, and information from cyber threats. By adhering to these lessons, we can build a secure and resilient digital ecosystem for future generations.

Examining Cybersecurity Strategies in Different Countries

In today's increasingly digital world, the importance of cybersecurity cannot be overstated. As technology advances, so do the threats that governments, businesses, and individuals face in the cyber realm. It is crucial for nations to develop robust cybersecurity strategies to safeguard their digital infrastructure, networks, and information from cyber threats. This subchapter delves into the examination of cybersecurity strategies adopted by different countries, providing an insightful analysis for teachers, politicians, scholars, academicians, journalists, observers, and diplomats.

One of the countries at the forefront of cybersecurity is the United States. With its vast technological advancements and a highly interconnected digital landscape, the U.S. has developed a multi-faceted approach to cybersecurity. The country emphasizes collaboration between government agencies, private sector entities, and international partners to share threat intelligence and coordinate responses. Additionally, the U.S. government invests heavily in research and development to stay ahead of emerging cyber threats.

China, on the other hand, has taken a different approach to cybersecurity. The Chinese government employs a more centralized model, heavily regulating the internet and implementing strict censorship policies. While this strategy has been effective in curbing cyber threats, it has also raised concerns about freedom of expression and privacy.

In Europe, the European Union (EU) has made significant strides in promoting cybersecurity across member states. The EU has established a comprehensive legal framework, including the General Data Protection Regulation (GDPR), to ensure the protection of personal data. The EU also prioritizes international cooperation and information sharing to combat cyber threats collectively.

In the Middle East, countries like Israel have become pioneers in cybersecurity. Due to its unique geopolitical situation and constant threats, Israel has developed one of the most advanced cybersecurity ecosystems in the world. The country invests heavily in research and development, fosters close collaboration between academia and industry, and encourages innovation in cybersecurity technologies.

Examining cybersecurity strategies in different countries provides valuable insights into the diverse approaches taken to protect digital infrastructure, networks, and information. By understanding these strategies, teachers can educate future generations on the importance of cybersecurity, politicians can shape policies to address emerging threats, scholars and academicians can further research in the field, journalists can report on global developments, observers can monitor progress, and diplomats can engage in international collaborations.

Overall, this subchapter serves as an essential resource for individuals interested in the niche of cybersecurity. It offers a comprehensive understanding of different countries' strategies, facilitating knowledge sharing and fostering a global dialogue on ensuring the security of information in the digital age.

Chapter 9: The Role of Teachers, Scholars, and Academicians in Cybersecurity Education

Importance of Cybersecurity Education

Subchapter: Importance of Cybersecurity Education

In today's digital age, where technology has become an integral part of our lives, the need for cybersecurity education cannot be overstated. As our dependence on digital infrastructure, networks, and information grows, so does the threat of cyber-attacks. It is imperative that we equip ourselves with the knowledge and skills required to safeguard our digital assets effectively. This subchapter explores the significance of cybersecurity education and its relevance to teachers, politicians, scholars, academicians, journalists, observers, and diplomats.

Cybersecurity education plays a pivotal role in addressing the ever-evolving landscape of cyber threats. Teachers can incorporate cybersecurity principles into their curriculum to foster a culture of cybersecurity awareness among students from an early age. By imparting knowledge about online safety, data privacy, and responsible digital citizenship, educators can empower the next generation to navigate the digital world securely.

For politicians, understanding the importance of cybersecurity education is crucial for developing effective policies and frameworks. Policymakers need to comprehend the intricacies of cyber threats and the potential consequences of their decisions on national security, economic stability, and individual privacy. By advocating for cybersecurity education initiatives, politicians can bridge the knowledge gap and better protect their constituents from cyber risks.

Scholars and academicians have a significant role to play in advancing cybersecurity education through research and innovation. By studying the latest trends and emerging technologies, they can contribute to the development of robust cybersecurity strategies and solutions. Moreover, academia can collaborate with industry experts to design comprehensive educational programs that equip students with the practical skills necessary to combat cyber threats effectively.

Journalists and observers, as the watchdogs of society, have a responsibility to inform the public about the importance of cybersecurity education. Through their reporting, they can raise awareness about cyber risks, highlight best practices, and expose vulnerabilities that may have far-reaching consequences. By educating themselves about cybersecurity principles, journalists can also protect their own digital communications and safeguard the integrity of their work.

Diplomats, in an interconnected world, must navigate complex cyber threats that transcend national borders. Cybersecurity education enables diplomats to understand the dynamics of cyber warfare, espionage, and attacks on critical infrastructure. By fostering international cooperation and knowledge exchange, diplomats can work towards establishing norms, treaties, and agreements that promote cybersecurity and protect global interests.

In conclusion, cybersecurity education is of paramount importance in today's digital age. It empowers individuals, institutions, and nations to defend against cyber threats effectively. Teachers, politicians, scholars, academicians, journalists, observers, and diplomats all have unique roles to play in advancing cybersecurity education. By prioritizing cybersecurity education, we can build a safer and more secure digital future for all.

Developing Cybersecurity Curricula

In an increasingly digitized world, where technology has become an integral part of everyday life, the need for robust cybersecurity measures has never been greater. As cyber threats continue to evolve and become more sophisticated, it is imperative that individuals, organizations, and governments equip themselves with the necessary knowledge and skills to protect their digital infrastructure, networks, and information. This subchapter, "Developing Cybersecurity Curricula," aims to provide valuable insights and guidance to teachers, politicians, scholars, academicians, journalists, observers, and diplomats on how to design and implement effective cybersecurity curricula.

As the demand for cybersecurity professionals is growing rapidly, it is essential for educational institutions to develop curricula that cover the diverse aspects of this field. The first step is to establish a strong foundation by educating students about the fundamental principles and concepts of cybersecurity. This includes topics such as threat landscape analysis, risk assessment, and ethical considerations in cybersecurity. Moreover, students should be exposed to the legal and regulatory frameworks relevant to cybersecurity, emphasizing the importance of compliance and accountability.

To ensure that the cybersecurity curricula remain relevant and up-to-date, it is crucial to incorporate hands-on practical experiences. This can be achieved through the integration of real-world case studies, simulations, and cybersecurity labs. By engaging students in practical exercises, they can develop the necessary technical skills to identify vulnerabilities, detect cyber threats, and implement effective countermeasures.

Collaboration between academia, industry, and government is vital in developing comprehensive cybersecurity curricula. This collaboration allows for the identification of emerging trends and the inclusion of the latest technologies and methodologies in the curriculum. Additionally, partnerships with cybersecurity experts and professionals can provide valuable insights into industry best practices and real-world challenges, enhancing the practical relevance of the curricula.

Furthermore, it is essential to promote multidisciplinary approaches in cybersecurity education. The field of cybersecurity intersects with various disciplines, including computer science, law, psychology, and international relations. By incorporating interdisciplinary perspectives into the curricula, students can develop a holistic understanding of cybersecurity issues, enabling them to tackle complex challenges in a comprehensive manner.

In conclusion, developing cybersecurity curricula is crucial for preparing individuals to safeguard digital infrastructure, networks, and information from cyber threats. This subchapter has provided a framework for teachers, politicians, scholars, academicians, journalists, observers, and diplomats to design effective curricula. By establishing a strong foundation, incorporating hands-on practical experiences, fostering collaboration, and promoting multidisciplinary approaches, cybersecurity education can empower individuals to protect against evolving cyber threats and contribute to a more secure digital age.

Training the Next Generation of Cybersecurity Professionals

In today's digital age, where cyber threats are becoming more sophisticated and prevalent, the need for well-trained cybersecurity professionals has never been greater. As the backbone of our digital infrastructure, networks, and information, it is crucial to ensure that these professionals are equipped with the knowledge and skills necessary to protect our valuable assets from malicious actors. This subchapter aims to shed light on the importance of training the next generation of cybersecurity professionals and offers insights into effective strategies to achieve this goal.

Teachers, politicians, scholars, academicians, journalists, observers, and diplomats alike play a pivotal role in shaping the future of cybersecurity. By recognizing the significance of this field, they can contribute to the development of comprehensive training programs and curricula that equip individuals with the necessary technical and analytical skills. Such programs should not only focus on theoretical knowledge but also provide hands-on experience through practical exercises and simulations, enabling future professionals to comprehend real-world scenarios and develop critical thinking capabilities.

One key aspect to consider in training the next generation of cybersecurity professionals is the need for interdisciplinary education. Cybersecurity is not solely a technical domain but requires a holistic approach that encompasses legal, ethical, and sociopolitical aspects. By integrating these elements into the curriculum, educators can produce well-rounded professionals who understand the broader implications of their actions and can navigate the complex landscape of cybersecurity with integrity and responsibility.

Furthermore, collaboration between academia, industry, and government institutions is crucial in preparing future cybersecurity professionals. By fostering partnerships and establishing mentorship programs, students can gain exposure to real-world challenges and industry best practices. This collaboration also enables the sharing of knowledge and expertise, ensuring that training programs remain up-to-date and relevant.

To address the evolving nature of cyber threats, continuous professional development and lifelong learning should be emphasized. The field of cybersecurity is constantly evolving, and professionals must stay updated with the latest trends, technologies, and countermeasures. This requires establishing mechanisms for ongoing training and certification, encouraging professionals to engage in research, and promoting participation in conferences and workshops.

In conclusion, training the next generation of cybersecurity professionals is of paramount importance in safeguarding our digital infrastructure, networks, and information. This subchapter has highlighted the significance of interdisciplinary education, collaboration between stakeholders, and the need for lifelong learning. It is imperative that teachers, politicians, scholars, academicians, journalists, observers, and diplomats recognize their role in shaping the future of cybersecurity and take proactive measures to ensure that we have a well-prepared workforce capable of combating cyber threats effectively. By investing in comprehensive training programs, we can fortify our digital defenses and secure our information in the digital age.

Research and Innovation in Cybersecurity

In today's digital age, where technology is deeply intertwined with our everyday lives, ensuring the security of our digital infrastructure, networks, and information has become of utmost importance. As cyber threats continue to evolve and become more sophisticated, it is crucial for individuals and organizations to stay abreast of the latest research and innovation in the field of cybersecurity. This subchapter aims to provide an overview of the ongoing efforts in research and innovation to combat cyber threats, addressing a wide range of audiences including teachers, politicians, scholars, academicians, journalists, observers, and diplomats.

In recent years, the field of cybersecurity has seen a tremendous surge in research and innovation. Governments, academic institutions, and private organizations are investing heavily in research projects to develop cutting-edge techniques and technologies that can effectively counter cyber threats. These research endeavors encompass various domains, including cryptography, network security, data protection, behavioral analytics, artificial intelligence, and machine learning.

One of the key focuses of cybersecurity research is enhancing the robustness of cryptographic systems. Cryptography plays a vital role in securing our digital communications and transactions. Researchers are constantly exploring new encryption algorithms and protocols that can withstand attacks from quantum computers and other emerging threats. Furthermore, efforts are being made to develop methods for secure and efficient key exchange, authentication, and secure multiparty computation.

Another area of active research is network security. With the proliferation of interconnected devices and the advent of the Internet of Things (IoT), securing networks has become increasingly complex. Researchers are exploring innovative techniques such as anomaly detection, intrusion detection and prevention systems, and secure routing protocols to safeguard network infrastructures from unauthorized access and malicious activities.

Additionally, the research community is focusing on data protection methodologies to ensure the confidentiality, integrity, and availability of sensitive information. This includes developing advanced techniques for data encryption, secure data storage, access control mechanisms, and secure data sharing and collaboration.

Behavioral analytics, artificial intelligence, and machine learning are also being extensively studied to detect and mitigate cyber threats in real-time. These techniques analyze patterns, anomalies, and user behavior to identify potential security breaches and take proactive measures to prevent attacks.

Overall, the field of cybersecurity research and innovation is thriving. It is crucial for teachers, politicians, scholars, academicians, journalists, observers, and diplomats to stay informed about the latest advancements in order to make informed decisions, develop effective policies, and educate the public on cybersecurity best practices. Collaboration between academia, industry, and government entities is necessary to ensure that research findings are translated into practical solutions and effectively implemented to protect our digital infrastructure, networks, and information from cyber threats.

Chapter 10: Cybersecurity Journalism and Reporting

The Role of Journalists in Raising Cybersecurity Awareness

In today's digital age, where technological advancements have become a double-edged sword, the role of journalists in raising cybersecurity awareness has never been more critical. As teachers, politicians, scholars, academicians, journalists, observers, diplomats, and individuals concerned about cybersecurity, we must acknowledge the power and influence that journalists possess to shape public opinion and understanding of this complex issue.

Cybersecurity, with its focus on protecting digital infrastructure, networks, and information from cyber threats, has become a pressing concern for governments, organizations, and individuals worldwide. The rapid pace of technological innovation, coupled with the increasing sophistication of cybercriminals, calls for a comprehensive approach to address this issue. Journalists play a pivotal role in this endeavor by acting as the bridge between technical jargon and the general public, translating complex concepts into easily understandable language.

As the frontline communicators, journalists have the power to educate, inform, and raise awareness about the risks and challenges posed by cyber threats. Through their investigative reporting, they can shed light on emerging cybersecurity issues, vulnerabilities in digital systems, and the consequences of cyberattacks. By providing real-life examples and case studies, journalists can help the public understand the potential impact of cyber threats on their daily lives, businesses, and even national security.

Furthermore, journalists can play a crucial role in holding governments, organizations, and individuals accountable for their cybersecurity practices. Through their investigative work, they can expose negligence, cover-ups, or inadequate measures taken to protect sensitive information. This can prompt policymakers to take necessary action, businesses to invest in robust cybersecurity measures, and individuals to adopt safer online practices.

Journalists also have the power to debunk myths and dispel misinformation surrounding cybersecurity. With the proliferation of fake news and disinformation campaigns, it is crucial to have credible sources providing accurate information. By fact-checking and verifying information, journalists can help combat the spread of false narratives and ensure that the public receives reliable guidance on cybersecurity practices.

In conclusion, the role of journalists in raising cybersecurity awareness cannot be overstated. Their ability to educate, inform, hold accountable; and debunk myths makes them invaluable allies in the fight against cyber threats. As teachers, politicians, scholars, academicians, journalists, observers, diplomats, and individuals concerned about cybersecurity, we must recognize the importance of supporting and encouraging journalists in their crucial role of raising awareness and promoting a safer digital world.

Ethical Reporting of Cybersecurity Incidents

In today's digital age, where technology plays a critical role in every aspect of our lives, the importance of cybersecurity cannot be overstated. As cyber threats continue to evolve and become more sophisticated, it is imperative that individuals and organizations remain vigilant in protecting their digital infrastructure, networks, and information. Equally important is the ethical reporting of cybersecurity incidents, as it ensures transparency, accountability, and the necessary steps to prevent future breaches.

This subchapter aims to address the ethical considerations associated with reporting cybersecurity incidents, providing insights and guidelines for teachers, politicians, scholars, academicians, journalists, observers, and diplomats. By understanding the ethical implications of reporting such incidents, these stakeholders can contribute to a safer digital ecosystem.

One of the fundamental ethical principles in reporting cybersecurity incidents is accuracy. It is essential for reporters to gather accurate information and verify its authenticity before disseminating it to the public. This ensures that the reported incident is not exaggerated or misrepresented, preventing unnecessary panic or damage to the reputation of individuals or organizations involved.

Transparency and accountability are also crucial in ethical reporting. When a cybersecurity incident occurs, it is important to promptly notify the affected individuals or organizations, as well as any relevant authorities. By doing so, the necessary measures can be taken to mitigate the impact of the incident and prevent further damage. This transparency also promotes trust between the public and the affected entities, fostering a sense of security and openness.

Another ethical consideration is the protection of privacy. When reporting cybersecurity incidents, it is essential to respect the privacy rights of individuals or organizations involved. Personal information should be handled with utmost care and sensitivity, ensuring that it is only shared when necessary and in accordance with applicable laws and regulations.

Furthermore, ethical reporting should also focus on raising awareness and educating the public. By providing accurate and comprehensive information about cybersecurity incidents, individuals can take proactive measures to enhance their own cybersecurity. This includes promoting good cyber hygiene practices, such as using strong passwords, regularly updating software, and being cautious of suspicious emails or links.

In conclusion, ethical reporting of cybersecurity incidents plays a vital role in safeguarding the digital ecosystem. By adhering to principles of accuracy, transparency, accountability, privacy protection, and public education, teachers, politicians, scholars, academicians, journalists, observers, and diplomats can contribute to a safer and more secure digital age. Together, we can build a resilient and trustworthy cyber landscape that protects our infrastructure, networks, and information from cyber threats.

Challenges and Opportunities in Cybersecurity Journalism

In today's interconnected world, where cyber threats pose a significant risk to digital infrastructure, networks, and information, cybersecurity journalism plays a crucial role in keeping the public informed and raising awareness about the evolving landscape of cyber threats. This subchapter explores the challenges and opportunities faced by journalists in this specialized field, with a focus on the unique responsibilities they carry in providing accurate and timely information to the public.

One of the major challenges in cybersecurity journalism is the constantly evolving nature of cyber threats. As technology advances, so do the tactics employed by cybercriminals and state-sponsored hackers. Journalists must stay up-to-date with the latest developments in order to effectively report on new threats and vulnerabilities. This requires continuous education and collaboration with cybersecurity experts, as well as access to reliable sources of information.

Additionally, journalists face the challenge of conveying complex technical information to a wide audience. Cybersecurity journalism should not only target experts but also be accessible to teachers, politicians, scholars, academicians, observers, diplomats, and the general public. Journalists must strike a balance between providing accurate and detailed information while also simplifying technical jargon to ensure that their reports are easily understood.

Moreover, ethical considerations are essential in cybersecurity journalism. Journalists must tread carefully when reporting on cyber incidents and breaches, as their coverage has the potential to impact public perception and potentially compromise ongoing investigations. They must also be mindful of avoiding sensationalism while maintaining the public's interest and understanding of the severity of cyber threats.

Despite these challenges, there are significant opportunities for cybersecurity journalism to make a positive impact. The increasing reliance on digital technology and the growing frequency of cyber attacks have created a demand for accurate and reliable reporting in this field. Journalists can play a crucial role in raising awareness and promoting cybersecurity best practices among individuals, organizations, and governments.

Furthermore, journalists have the opportunity to hold governments and corporations accountable for their cybersecurity practices. By investigating and reporting on data breaches, vulnerabilities, and the effectiveness of cybersecurity measures, journalists can contribute to the improvement of cybersecurity strategies and policies.

In conclusion, cybersecurity journalism faces various challenges, including the dynamic nature of cyber threats, the need for accessibility, and ethical considerations. However, with these challenges come significant opportunities to inform, educate, and promote accountability in the realm of cybersecurity. By providing accurate and timely information, journalists can contribute to the protection of digital infrastructure, networks, and information in the digital age.

Collaborative Efforts between Journalists and Cybersecurity Professionals

In the digital age, where information flows freely and rapidly, the need for collaboration between journalists and cybersecurity professionals has become more crucial than ever. This subchapter explores the symbiotic relationship between these two domains and emphasizes the importance of their collaboration in securing information in the digital realm.

Journalists, as the fourth estate, play a vital role in ensuring transparency, accountability, and the flow of information in society. However, their work is not without risks. In an era where cyber threats are constantly evolving, journalists often find themselves targeted by hackers, state-sponsored actors, or other malicious entities seeking to compromise their sources, manipulate information, or undermine public trust. This necessitates the involvement of cybersecurity professionals who can provide guidance and support to journalists in safeguarding their digital infrastructure, networks, and information.

Cybersecurity professionals bring their expertise in identifying, mitigating, and responding to cyber threats. By collaborating with journalists, they can help establish secure communication channels, educate them on best practices for protecting their digital assets, and develop robust cyber defense strategies. This collaboration ensures that journalists can continue their crucial work without compromising their sources or the integrity of the information they disseminate.

For journalists, understanding the fundamentals of cybersecurity is paramount. They must be aware of the risks associated with digital communication, such as phishing attacks, malware, or social engineering. By partnering with cybersecurity professionals, journalists can gain insights into the latest cyber threats, learn to recognize suspicious activities, and adopt effective security measures to protect their digital platforms.

On the other hand, cybersecurity professionals can benefit from collaborating with journalists. Journalists often possess extensive knowledge of current events, geopolitical dynamics, and emerging trends. This information can be invaluable in helping cybersecurity professionals identify potential threats, anticipate new attack vectors, and stay ahead of cybercriminals. Journalists can also provide a broader context for cybersecurity incidents, helping to bridge the gap between technical jargon and public understanding.

In conclusion, the collaboration between journalists and cybersecurity professionals is essential in securing information in the digital age. This partnership enables journalists to continue their crucial role as watchdogs of society, while also ensuring that they are equipped with the necessary tools and knowledge to navigate the digital landscape safely. By working together, journalists and cybersecurity professionals can strengthen the integrity of information, foster public trust, and contribute to a more secure digital environment.

Chapter 11: Observing and Analyzing Cyber Threats

Cyber Intelligence Gathering and Analysis

In today's digital age, where information is a valuable asset, the need to secure it from cyber threats has become paramount. Cybersecurity, a field that focuses on protecting digital infrastructure, networks, and information, plays a crucial role in safeguarding sensitive data and preventing potential breaches. One of the key components of effective cybersecurity is cyber intelligence gathering and analysis.

Cyber intelligence gathering involves the collection of valuable information about potential threats, adversaries, and vulnerabilities. It encompasses various techniques such as open-source intelligence, social engineering, and network monitoring. By gathering intelligence, organizations can gain insights into the tactics, techniques, and procedures employed by cybercriminals, enabling them to strengthen their defenses and stay one step ahead of potential threats.

Once the intelligence is collected, it needs to be analyzed to extract actionable insights. Cyber intelligence analysis involves the evaluation, processing, and interpretation of gathered data to identify patterns, trends, and potential risks. Skilled analysts use their expertise to connect the dots and make sense of the vast amounts of information collected. This analysis helps organizations develop effective strategies, prioritize resources, and make informed decisions to protect their digital assets.

For teachers, politicians, scholars, academicians, journalists, observers, and diplomats, understanding the importance of cyber intelligence gathering and analysis is crucial. With the rapid advancement of technology, cyber threats are evolving at an alarming rate, posing significant risks to national security, economic stability, and individual privacy. By familiarizing themselves with cyber intelligence practices, these individuals can contribute to the development of robust cybersecurity policies and practices.

Teachers can incorporate cyber intelligence concepts into their curricula to educate the younger generation about the importance of cybersecurity and the potential risks associated with the digital world. Politicians and diplomats can utilize cyber intelligence to inform their decision-making processes and develop effective legislation and international agreements to combat cyber threats. Scholars and academicians can conduct research in the field of cyber intelligence to advance knowledge and propose innovative solutions. Journalists and observers can use cyber intelligence to report on emerging cyber threats and raise public awareness.

In conclusion, cyber intelligence gathering and analysis is a critical aspect of cybersecurity. By collecting and analyzing relevant information about potential threats, organizations can proactively protect their digital infrastructure, networks, and information. For teachers, politicians, scholars, academicians, journalists, observers, and diplomats, understanding and incorporating cyber intelligence concepts is vital in addressing the ever-growing challenges in the digital age. By working together, we can secure information and ensure a safer digital future.

Tools and Techniques for Cyber Threat Monitoring

In today's interconnected digital age, the importance of cybersecurity cannot be overstated. As technology continues to evolve, so do the threats that target our digital infrastructure, networks, and information. To effectively protect against these cyber threats, individuals and organizations must adopt proactive monitoring practices and utilize the right tools and techniques. This subchapter explores various tools and techniques for cyber threat monitoring, providing valuable insights for teachers, politicians, scholars, academicians, journalists, observers, diplomats, and anyone interested in cybersecurity.

1. Intrusion Detection Systems (IDS): IDS tools are essential for monitoring network traffic and identifying potential threats or anomalies. They analyze data packets, monitor system logs, and raise alerts when suspicious activity is detected. IDS can be either network-based or host-based, providing comprehensive monitoring capabilities.

2. Security Information and Event Management (SIEM): SIEM tools collect and analyze logs from various sources, including firewalls, servers, and network devices. By aggregating and correlating this data, SIEM systems provide a holistic view of an organization's security posture, enabling real-time threat monitoring and incident response.

3. Threat Intelligence Platforms: These platforms leverage advanced analytics and machine learning algorithms to gather, analyze, and disseminate threat intelligence. They help organizations stay up to date with the latest cyber threats, identify potential risks, and take proactive measures to prevent attacks.

4. Vulnerability Assessment Tools: These tools scan networks, systems, and applications to identify weaknesses that could be exploited by cybercriminals. By regularly conducting vulnerability assessments, organizations can proactively address security flaws and prevent potential breaches.

5. Security Operations Centers (SOC): A SOC is a centralized unit responsible for monitoring, detecting, analyzing, and responding to cybersecurity incidents. It combines people, processes, and technology to provide continuous monitoring and rapid incident response.

6. Threat Hunting: This proactive technique involves actively searching for threats that may bypass traditional security controls. Threat hunters use various tools and techniques to identify and mitigate advanced persistent threats (APTs) and other sophisticated attacks.

7. Data Loss Prevention (DLP) Solutions: DLP tools monitor and control data in motion, at rest, and in use to prevent unauthorized access, leakage, or theft. These solutions help organizations protect sensitive information and comply with data privacy regulations.

By adopting these tools and techniques for cyber threat monitoring, teachers, politicians, scholars, academicians, journalists, observers, diplomats, and individuals in the cybersecurity niche can enhance their understanding and defense against evolving cyber threats. Remember, effective cybersecurity is a collective responsibility, and staying informed about the latest tools and techniques is crucial in this rapidly changing digital landscape.

Assessing the Impact of Cyber Threats

In today's digital age, the rapidly advancing technology has brought about countless conveniences and opportunities. However, it has also given rise to a new breed of threats - cyber threats. These threats pose a significant risk to our digital infrastructure, networks, and information. In this subchapter, we will delve into assessing the impact of cyber threats and shed light on their implications for the various stakeholders, including teachers, politicians, scholars, academicians, journalists, observers, and diplomats.

For teachers, understanding the impact of cyber threats is crucial as they play a vital role in educating the younger generation. By comprehending the consequences of cyber threats, teachers can equip students with the necessary knowledge and skills to navigate the digital landscape safely. They can incorporate cybersecurity awareness into their curriculum, teaching students about online safety, responsible digital citizenship, and the potential repercussions of cyberattacks.

Politicians hold the responsibility of enacting policies and legislation that safeguard the digital infrastructure of a nation. By assessing the impact of cyber threats, politicians can develop robust cybersecurity frameworks and allocate resources effectively. They can collaborate with experts to draft laws that deter cybercriminals, while also promoting international cooperation to combat cyber threats collectively.

Scholars and academicians can contribute significantly to the field of cybersecurity by conducting research on the impact of cyber threats. By analyzing the consequences of cyberattacks on different sectors, they can identify vulnerabilities and propose effective countermeasures. Their findings can guide policymakers, organizations, and individuals in adopting proactive strategies and developing resilient systems against cyber threats.

Journalists and observers have a crucial role in disseminating information about cyber threats to the public. By reporting on cyber incidents and their implications, they can raise awareness and foster a culture of cyber resilience. Journalists can highlight the importance of cybersecurity practices, alert the public about emerging threats, and hold organizations accountable for protecting sensitive information.

Diplomats, in their pursuit of international relations, must understand the impact of cyber threats on a global scale. By assessing the consequences of cyberattacks, diplomats can engage in diplomatic dialogues to establish norms, rules, and cooperation frameworks that address cybersecurity challenges effectively. They can work towards building trust, promoting information sharing, and mitigating the potential risks associated with cyber threats.

In conclusion, assessing the impact of cyber threats is essential for various stakeholders in the realms of education, politics, academia, media, observation, and diplomacy. By comprehending the implications of cyber threats, these individuals can contribute to the development of robust cybersecurity measures, raise awareness, and foster a safer digital environment for all.

Predicting and Preventing Future Cyber Attacks

In today's digital age, where technology pervades every aspect of our lives, ensuring the security of our information has become more critical than ever. With the increasing prevalence of cyber threats, it is imperative for individuals and organizations to stay ahead of the game by predicting and preventing future cyber attacks.

This subchapter focuses on the field of cybersecurity, which is dedicated to protecting digital infrastructure, networks, and information from cyber threats. It aims to provide teachers, politicians, scholars, academicians, journalists, observers, and diplomats with a comprehensive understanding of the strategies and tools available to predict and prevent future cyber attacks.

To effectively predict future cyber attacks, knowledge of past attacks is essential. By analyzing historical attack patterns and trends, cybersecurity professionals can gain valuable insights into the methods and techniques employed by hackers. This knowledge enables them to anticipate potential vulnerabilities and devise countermeasures to mitigate future attacks.

One of the key tools used in predicting future cyber attacks is threat intelligence. By monitoring and analyzing data from various sources, such as security reports, online forums, and dark web marketplaces, cybersecurity experts can identify emerging threats and adapt their defense strategies accordingly. Additionally, collaboration and information-sharing among organizations and governments play a crucial role in staying ahead of cybercriminals.

Preventing future cyber attacks requires a multi-layered approach. This includes implementing robust security measures, such as firewalls, intrusion detection systems, and encryption, to protect digital infrastructure and networks. Regular vulnerability assessments and penetration testing can help identify weak points and address them before they are exploited by cybercriminals.

Education and awareness are also vital in preventing cyber attacks. By providing training and resources to individuals and organizations, they can learn best practices for securing their digital assets and become less susceptible to cyber threats. Governments can play a significant role by creating policies and regulations that promote cybersecurity and incentivize organizations to prioritize security measures.

Furthermore, technological advancements, such as artificial intelligence and machine learning, hold great potential in predicting and preventing future cyber attacks. These technologies can analyze vast amounts of data in real-time, detect anomalies, and automatically respond to potential threats, thus enhancing the overall security posture.

In conclusion, predicting and preventing future cyber attacks is a continuous process that requires a proactive approach. By leveraging threat intelligence, implementing robust security measures, promoting education and awareness, and embracing technological advancements, we can stay one step ahead of cybercriminals. It is crucial for teachers, politicians, scholars, academicians, journalists, observers, and diplomats to understand the significance of cybersecurity and work together to secure information in the digital age.

Chapter 12: Diplomatic Approaches to Cybersecurity

Cyber Diplomacy and International Relations

In today's interconnected world, where the internet plays a pivotal role in every aspect of our lives, including politics and diplomacy, the concept of cyber diplomacy has emerged as a crucial component of international relations. This subchapter explores the significance of cyber diplomacy and its implications for the global community. It aims to equip teachers, politicians, scholars, academicians, journalists, observers, and diplomats with a comprehensive understanding of this rapidly evolving field.

Cyber diplomacy refers to the use of diplomatic channels and negotiations to address issues related to cybersecurity, digital infrastructure, and information protection. As cyber threats continue to evolve and become more sophisticated, it is imperative for nations to collaborate and engage in cyber diplomacy to ensure a secure and stable digital environment.

This subchapter delves into the key principles and practices of cyber diplomacy, focusing on its role in international relations. It discusses the importance of building trust and fostering cooperation among nations to effectively address cyber threats on a global scale. It explores the challenges that arise in cyberspace, such as attribution and the lack of universally accepted norms, and provides insights into how cyber diplomacy can overcome these hurdles.

Furthermore, this subchapter highlights the role of international organizations, such as the United Nations and regional bodies, in shaping cyber diplomacy and fostering dialogue among nations. It delves into the efforts of these organizations in creating frameworks and guidelines for responsible state behavior in cyberspace.

The content also explores case studies and real-world examples of cyber diplomacy in action. It analyzes notable incidents of cyber attacks and the diplomatic responses employed to mitigate their impacts. By examining these cases, the readers gain a deeper understanding of the challenges faced by diplomats and the potential for cyber diplomacy to shape international relations.

In conclusion, this subchapter provides a comprehensive overview of cyber diplomacy and its significance in the realm of international relations. It equips teachers, politicians, scholars, academicians, journalists, observers, and diplomats with the knowledge and insights necessary to navigate the complex landscape of cybersecurity and effectively engage in cyber diplomacy. By fostering a deeper understanding and promoting cooperation, cyber diplomacy has the potential to strengthen the global community's ability to address the ever-evolving cyber threats.

Cybersecurity Cooperation between Nations

In an increasingly interconnected world, the need for international cooperation in cybersecurity has become paramount. As societies become more reliant on digital infrastructure, networks, and information, the threat of cyber attacks has also grown exponentially. This subchapter, "Cybersecurity Cooperation between Nations," aims to shed light on the importance of collaborative efforts between countries to combat cyber threats and protect our digital age.

In today's interconnected world, a cyber attack against one nation can have far-reaching consequences for others. The interconnectedness of global networks means that vulnerabilities in one country's digital infrastructure can be exploited by adversaries from anywhere in the world. This calls for a collective response, where nations cooperate to exchange information, share best practices, and develop common strategies to counter cyber threats effectively.

Cybersecurity cooperation between nations is not only crucial for protecting national security but also for safeguarding economic stability and ensuring the privacy and safety of citizens. By working together, countries can create a unified front against cybercriminals, state-sponsored hackers, and other malicious actors who seek to exploit vulnerabilities in digital systems.

This subchapter will explore various aspects of cybersecurity cooperation between nations, including:

1. Information sharing: The exchange of timely and relevant information about cyber threats is vital for effective cybersecurity. This subchapter will delve into the importance of sharing threat intelligence, incident response capabilities, and best practices among nations.

2. International legal frameworks: International agreements and legal frameworks play a crucial role in fostering cybersecurity cooperation. This section will discuss the importance of bilateral and multilateral agreements, as well as the role of international organizations in facilitating cooperation and establishing norms of responsible behavior in cyberspace.

3. Capacity building: Developing cybersecurity capabilities is essential for nations to effectively respond to cyber threats. This subchapter will highlight the significance of capacity building programs, such as knowledge sharing, training, and technical assistance, to strengthen the cybersecurity posture of nations, particularly those with limited resources.

4. Public-private partnerships: Collaboration between governments and the private sector is vital in addressing cybersecurity challenges.

This section will explore the role of public-private partnerships in sharing expertise, resources, and technological innovations to enhance cybersecurity defenses.

By addressing these key areas, this subchapter aims to provide a comprehensive understanding of the importance of cybersecurity cooperation between nations. It is intended to serve as a valuable resource for teachers, politicians, scholars, academicians, journalists, observers, and diplomats interested in the field of cybersecurity. Together, through international collaboration, we can secure information in the digital age and build a safer and more resilient digital future.

Diplomatic Efforts to Establish Cyber Norms

In an increasingly interconnected world, where cyber threats have become a major concern for governments, organizations, and individuals, establishing cyber norms has become essential. This subchapter delves into the diplomatic efforts made to establish these norms and highlights their significance in securing information in the digital age.

Cybersecurity, with its focus on protecting digital infrastructure, networks, and information from cyber threats, has become a pressing issue. To address this challenge, diplomatic efforts have been underway to establish global standards and norms that govern state behavior in cyberspace.

One of the key diplomatic initiatives in this regard is the United Nations Group of Governmental Experts (UN GGE) on Developments in the Field of Information and Telecommunications in the Context of International Security. Comprising representatives from various countries, the UN GGE has been instrumental in shaping cyber norms. Its work has resulted in reports that outline principles and guidelines for responsible state behavior in cyberspace.

Furthermore, regional organizations such as the European Union (EU) and the African Union (AU) have also taken significant steps in establishing cyber norms. The EU Cybersecurity Strategy, for instance, emphasizes the need for a secure and resilient cyberspace while promoting norms of responsible state behavior. Similarly, the AU Convention on Cyber Security and Personal Data Protection aims to harmonize cybersecurity efforts across African nations and establish norms for information sharing and cooperation.

These diplomatic efforts have been crucial in fostering international cooperation and dialogue on cyber norms. They have facilitated discussions on issues such as cyber warfare, hacking, data breaches, and the protection of critical infrastructure. By setting norms, these efforts seek to create a more predictable and stable cyberspace where countries can engage in responsible behavior and mitigate potential cyber risks.

It is paramount for teachers, politicians, scholars, academicians, journalists, observers, and diplomats to be aware of these diplomatic efforts and their implications. They play a vital role in shaping public opinion, policy formulation, and international relations. By understanding the intricacies of cyber norms and the diplomatic efforts behind them, these stakeholders can contribute to the development of effective cybersecurity strategies and policies.

In conclusion, the establishment of cyber norms through diplomatic efforts is crucial in securing information in the digital age. The UN GGE, regional organizations like the EU and AU, and other diplomatic initiatives have played a pivotal role in shaping these norms. By familiarizing themselves with these efforts, teachers, politicians, scholars, academicians, journalists, observers, and diplomats can actively contribute to the ongoing discussions and work towards a safer and more secure cyberspace.

Multilateral Organizations and Cybersecurity Diplomacy

In today's interconnected world, where cyberspace plays an increasingly crucial role in our daily lives, the need for robust cybersecurity measures has never been more pressing. As nations grapple with the challenges posed by cyber threats, the role of multilateral organizations in fostering cybersecurity diplomacy has become paramount. This subchapter explores the significance of these organizations in addressing the evolving landscape of digital security and highlights their efforts in promoting international cooperation and information sharing.

Multilateral organizations, such as the United Nations (UN), the International Telecommunication Union (ITU), and the North Atlantic Treaty Organization (NATO), among others, play a vital role in facilitating cybersecurity diplomacy. These organizations serve as platforms for nations to collaborate, exchange best practices, and harmonize policies to counter cyber threats effectively.

The UN, through its various specialized agencies, has been at the forefront of fostering international cooperation in cybersecurity. The UN Group of Governmental Experts on Developments in the Field of Information and Telecommunications in the Context of International Security (UN GGE) has been instrumental in shaping norms and rules for responsible state behavior in cyberspace. By engaging in dialogue and negotiations, the UN GGE has laid the foundation for building trust and confidence among nations, ultimately leading to a more secure digital environment.

The ITU, as the specialized agency of the UN for information and communication technologies (ICTs), focuses on developing global standards and guidelines for cybersecurity. This includes promoting capacity-building programs to bridge the digital divide and enhance the cybersecurity capabilities of developing nations. Through its efforts, the ITU aims to create a harmonized and secure digital ecosystem that benefits all.

NATO, primarily known for its collective defense in the physical realm, recognizes the growing significance of cybersecurity in the modern threat landscape. The organization has established a Cyber Defense Pledge, committing member states to enhance their cyber defense capabilities and promote information sharing. NATO's Cooperative Cyber Defense Center of Excellence (CCDCOE) serves as a hub for research, training, and analysis, further strengthening the collective resilience against cyber threats.

For teachers, politicians, scholars, academicians, journalists, observers, and diplomats, understanding the role of multilateral organizations in cybersecurity diplomacy is crucial. These organizations provide a platform for knowledge exchange, policy development, and coordination among nations. By highlighting the efforts of these organizations, this subchapter aims to raise awareness of the importance of international cooperation in securing information in the digital age.

In conclusion, as the threat landscape in cyberspace continues to evolve, effective cybersecurity diplomacy becomes indispensable. Multilateral organizations play a vital role in fostering international cooperation, establishing norms, and sharing best practices. By engaging in cybersecurity diplomacy, nations can collectively address cyber threats and ensure a safer digital environment for all.

Chapter 13: Conclusion

Recap of Key Concepts and Takeaways

In this subchapter, we will summarize the fundamental concepts and key takeaways covered throughout the book "Securing Information in the Digital Age: A Comprehensive Handbook for Politicians and Diplomats." This recap is intended for teachers, politicians, scholars, academicians, journalists, observers, diplomats, and anyone interested in the niche of cybersecurity, which focuses on protecting digital infrastructure, networks, and information from cyber threats.

1. Understanding the Cybersecurity Landscape:

We explored the evolving nature of cyber threats and the importance of recognizing the interconnectedness of digital systems. Key takeaways include the need for a proactive approach to cybersecurity, considering the human factor, and staying updated on emerging threats.

2. Building a Secure Digital Infrastructure:

We emphasized the significance of robust digital infrastructure and the role of policymakers in enacting regulations and standards to ensure its security. Key concepts covered include encryption, secure coding practices, multi-factor authentication, and regular system updates.

3. Protecting Networks from Cyber Attacks:

This section delved into strategies for safeguarding networks from cyber attacks. Key takeaways include implementing firewalls, intrusion detection and prevention systems, and conducting regular vulnerability assessments. Additionally, creating incident response plans and fostering a culture of security awareness are crucial.

4. Safeguarding Information Assets:

We discussed the importance of protecting sensitive information from unauthorized access or disclosure. Key concepts covered include data classification, access controls, encryption, and secure data storage and transfer. Takeaways include the need for robust authentication mechanisms and the use of strong, unique passwords.

5. International Cooperation in Cybersecurity:

Recognizing that cyber threats transcend national boundaries, we explored the importance of international cooperation in addressing cybersecurity challenges. Key takeaways include the need for information sharing, collaborative frameworks, and diplomatic efforts to establish norms and deter malicious cyber activities.

6. The Role of Education and Awareness:

We highlighted the significance of education and awareness in promoting cybersecurity practices. Takeaways include the need for cybersecurity training programs, public awareness campaigns, and fostering a culture of cybersecurity within organizations and society as a whole.

In conclusion, this subchapter provided a comprehensive recap of key concepts and takeaways from the book "Securing Information in the Digital Age." It underscored the importance of a proactive approach to cybersecurity, building secure digital infrastructure, protecting networks and information assets, international cooperation, and promoting education and awareness. By embracing these concepts, teachers, politicians, scholars, academicians, journalists, observers, and diplomats can contribute to a safer digital environment and better protect against cyber threats.

The Ongoing Battle for Cybersecurity

In today's digital age, the world is becoming increasingly interconnected, making cybersecurity a pressing concern for individuals, organizations, and governments alike. The rapid advancements in technology have brought about numerous benefits, but they have also given rise to new and sophisticated cyber threats that can compromise our digital infrastructure, networks, and sensitive information. This subchapter delves into the ongoing battle for cybersecurity, examining its importance, challenges, and the strategies required to tackle this ever-evolving threat landscape.

Cybersecurity is not just a technical issue; it is a multidimensional problem that requires a comprehensive approach. Teachers, politicians, scholars, academicians, journalists, observers, and diplomats play a crucial role in understanding, advocating, and implementing effective cybersecurity policies and practices. Their collective efforts can contribute to building a resilient and secure digital world.

One of the primary challenges in the ongoing battle for cybersecurity is the constantly evolving nature of cyber threats. Hackers and cybercriminals are continually adapting and developing new techniques to breach defenses, making it essential for policymakers and practitioners to stay ahead of the curve. This subchapter explores the dynamic landscape of cyber threats, including malware, phishing attacks, ransomware, and state-sponsored cyber espionage, while providing insights into their potential impact on societies and economies.

To effectively protect digital infrastructure and information, collaboration and information sharing are vital. The subchapter emphasizes the need for cooperation among governments, organizations, and individuals to combat cyber threats effectively. It highlights the importance of international agreements, such as bilateral cybersecurity partnerships and multilateral frameworks, in fostering global cybersecurity resilience.

Furthermore, the subchapter delves into the role of education and awareness in promoting cybersecurity. Teachers and academicians have the responsibility to educate and equip the next generation with the necessary knowledge and skills to navigate the digital landscape safely. Policymakers and diplomats can advocate for the inclusion of cybersecurity in educational curricula and promote public awareness campaigns to encourage responsible digital behavior.

In conclusion, the battle for cybersecurity is an ongoing struggle that requires collective efforts from various stakeholders. Teachers, politicians, scholars, academicians, journalists, observers, and diplomats have a crucial role in understanding the complexities of cyber threats and advocating for effective cybersecurity policies. By fostering collaboration, promoting education, and raising awareness, we can build a safer and more secure digital age for all.

Empowering Politicians and Diplomats in Securing Information in the Digital Age.

Empowering Politicians and Diplomats in Securing Information in the Digital Age

In today's interconnected world, where technology plays a crucial role in every aspect of our lives, the need to secure information has become paramount. This is particularly true for politicians and diplomats, who hold sensitive and confidential information that, if compromised, could have far-reaching consequences. In this subchapter, we will explore strategies and tools that empower politicians and diplomats in securing information in the digital age.

With the rise of cyber threats, it is imperative for politicians and diplomats to understand the importance of cybersecurity. By focusing on protecting digital infrastructure, networks, and information, they can effectively safeguard their communications and data from malicious actors. This subchapter aims to provide them with comprehensive insights and practical guidance to enhance their cybersecurity posture.

To begin, we will delve into the current landscape of cyber threats, examining the various types of attacks that politicians and diplomats may face. By understanding the tactics employed by hackers, they can better anticipate and mitigate potential risks. We will also explore case studies and real-world examples to illustrate the consequences of information breaches and the lessons learned from such incidents.

A key aspect of empowering politicians and diplomats in securing information is education and awareness. We will discuss the importance of training programs that equip them with the necessary knowledge and skills to identify and respond to cyber threats. This includes understanding best practices for password management, recognizing phishing attempts, and employing encryption techniques.

Furthermore, we will discuss the role of technology in enhancing information security. Topics such as secure communication platforms, encryption algorithms, and secure data storage solutions will be explored. By leveraging the right tools and technologies, politicians and diplomats can ensure the confidentiality, integrity, and availability of their information.

The subchapter will also address the importance of collaboration and international cooperation in securing information. Given the transnational nature of cyber threats, politicians and diplomats must work together to share information, exchange best practices, and develop common frameworks for cybersecurity.

In conclusion, "Empowering Politicians and Diplomats in Securing Information in the Digital Age" highlights the critical role that politicians and diplomats play in protecting sensitive information. By understanding the evolving landscape of cyber threats, investing in education and training, leveraging technology, and fostering collaboration, they can effectively secure their communications and data in the digital age. This subchapter serves as a comprehensive resource for teachers, politicians, scholars, academicians, journalists, observers, and diplomats interested in the niche of cybersecurity.